BEST TRAILS
IN and AROUND
KARTCHNER CAVERNS STATE PARK®

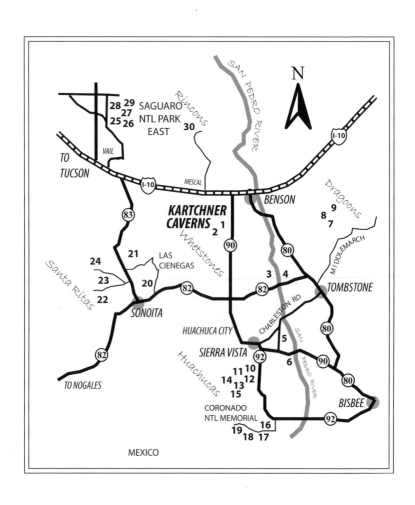

N

I-10

TO TUCSON

VAIL

28 29
27
25 26

SAGUARO
NTL PARK
EAST

30

Rincons

SAN PEDRO RIVER

I-10

MESCAL

BENSON

Dragoons

83

KARTCHNER
CAVERNS
2 1

9
8 7

90

80

MIDDLEMARCH

24

21

LAS
CIENEGAS

Whetstones

3 4

Santa Ritas

23

22

20

82

82

CHARLESTON RD

TOMBSTONE

SONOITA

HUACHUCA CITY

SAN PEDRO RIVER

80

82

SIERRA VISTA

5

92

6

90

80

TO NOGALES

Huachucas

11 10
14 12
13
15

BISBEE

CORONADO
NTL MEMORIAL

16

92

19 18 17

MEXICO

BEST TRAILS

IN AND AROUND

KARTCHNER CAVERNS STATE PARK

A Guide for Hikers, Bicyclists and Equestrians

Kelly Tighe

Best Trails Publishing
Bisbee, Arizona

BEST TRAILS PUBLISHING

P.O. Box 1831, Bisbee, AZ 85603
(520) 432-5242 · ktighe@theriver.com

Book design: Slim Tighe
Cartography: Slim Tighe
Front cover photograph: A hiker makes his way along Carr Peak Trail.
Photographs: Kelly and Slim Tighe except where noted otherwise.

Kartchner Caverns State Park® is a federally registered trademark. The name is used in the book's title, and throughout the text, with permission of Arizona State Parks.

WARNING: Some of the trails described in this book pass through exceedingly rugged and remote country. The extremes in temperature, presence of poisonous animals and scarcity of water are all things to be considered when planning your trip. It is the user's responsibility to decide whether you possess the skills and physical fitness required for each trip. Judgements regarding trail and weather conditions are also the responsibility of the user. The author, publisher and all those associated with this publication, directly or indirectly, disclaim any liability for accidents, injuries, damages or losses that may occur to anyone using this book.

Printed in the United States of America

Library of Congress Control Number: 2002102852

ISBN 0-9711437-4-9

CONTENTS

ACKNOWLEDGMENTS

SPECIAL THANKS to my husband, Slim Tighe, for his encouragement and his assistance in hiking, photography, cartography, book production and layout.

Thanks to friends who helped scout the trails: Annette Cordano, Debra Wright, Larry Prevett, Jan Edgerton, Lil Leclerc, Kate Ladson, Jan Dillon, Garrett and Ryan Dillon, and my horse, Manchado.

Thanks to the following for technical information:
Kelly Darnall, Kartchner Caverns State Park;
Scott Sticha, Barbara Alberti, Coronado National Memorial;
Joan Vassey, Coronado National Forest Sierra Vista Ranger District;
Les Dufour, Coronado National Forest Douglas Ranger District;
Jane Childress, Bureau of Land Management Sierra Vista Field Office;
Catie Fenn, Bureau of Land Management Tucson Field Office;
Bob Lineback and Melani Florez, Saguaro National Park;
Mark Pretti, Ramsey Canyon Preserve;
Dutch Nagle, Friends of the San Pedro;
Leonard Taylor, author of *Discover the San Pedro Valley* and *Hikers Guide to the Huachuca Mountains;*
Kathleen Manton, Arizona Lithographers;
Patricia Reinhold, Proofing;
Mike White, Ghost River Images.

Thanks to Stan Young for *Quail Sisters* and thanks to Bryan Lee, Pam Gluck and Marty Cordano for their thoughtful words on the back cover of this book.

QUAIL SISTERS

The quail sisters meet every morning in the desert,
they wear those question marks upon their heads.
They'll gather into circles and talk of seeds and blossoms,
sometimes I can hear 'em hear from my bed
As they dance through every rumor, as chicks are bein' fed,
they'll scratch on every topic and though it's all been said,
Our quail sisters meet every morning in the desert.
They all wear question marks upon their heads.

Señor Coyote's fascinated, even when he isn't hungry,
as they gossip while he's napping in the weeds.
How can they seem so happy with their scratching and their chatter
never ever scratching any deeper than they need?
Sometimes when he's jealous he'll set them all a'fright,
dashes out to trash the meeting...he shatters morning light.
And when our quail sisters meet next morning in the desert
they show those question marks upon their heads.

Us coyotes...we get together each evening in the desert.
We'll sigh about the weather and the faces of the moon.
It's been our nightly habit to discuss the lack of rabbits,
but even when we're hungry, there'll be time to wail a tune.
There's the hunting and the craving, and always pups to teach,
There's the yearning and the raving for all beyond our reach.
And still our quail sisters meet every morning in the desert.
They all wear question marks upon their heads.

Pat Maloney and Stan Young

Entrance to Kartchner Caverns State Park

INTRODUCTION

Few places can boast the environmental and historical diversity that is found within a forty-mile radius of Kartchner Caverns State Park.

The park, located in the foothills of the Whetstone Mountains of southeastern Arizona, is the centerpiece of a truly remarkable variety of trail opportunities. From classic Sonoran Desert to forested mountaintop trails, to ghost towns and Apache hideouts, there is something for everyone.

If the reader hikes the trails from 1 to 30 as described in this book, the Whetstone Range is visible from east, south, west and north in a clockwise rotation. *BEST TRAILS* has trail information for hikers, bicyclists and equestrians, as well as several barrier-free, wheelchair accessible trails. Many of the trails are easy enough for families with small children.

The San Pedro Valley, east of the Whetstones, has been a haven for humans and wildlife for thousands of years. Thirteen thousand years ago people from the Clovis Culture hunted mammoths and other Ice Age animals in the area.

In 1776 the King of Spain established a fort along the San Pedro River. Disintegrating remains of the 200 year-old adobe walls are still visible, on a high bluff overlooking the river.

Beyond the San Pedro River, the pink, wind-sculpted pinnacles of the Dragoon Mountains northeast of Tombstone, mark the final resting place of the famous Apache leader, Cochise. Cochise died in 1874 and according to legend is buried in a secret place somewhere in the Dragoon Mountains.

The Huachuca Mountains, south of Kartchner Caverns State Park, are an excellent example of a southwestern "sky island". These beautiful mountains rise from the surrounding grasslands of the Chihuahuan Desert to the towering heights of 9,466-foot Miller Peak, which is often snow-capped in the winter months. Ramsey Canyon Preserve, tucked into a canyon on the east side of the range, offers information about some of the rare plants and animals that are found in the Huachucas.

Along the Mexico/United States border, on the southern end of the Huachuca range, Coronado National Memorial was established to commemorate Francisco Vasquez de Coronado's amazing journey of 1540, the first major exploration of Europeans into what is now the American Southwest.

The area surrounding Kartchner Caverns State Park has a mining history dating back to the Spanish who mined silver for the kings of Spain. Prospectors have blasted and tunneled the land in their search for silver, copper and gold. In the late 1800s and early 1900s small communities, such as Fairbank, along the San Pedro River and Kentucky Camp, in the foothills of the Santa Rita Mountains, developed to support the mining activities.

Northwest of Kartchner Caverns State Park two deserts intermingle as the Chihuahuan Desert blends into the Sonoran. Here, Saguaro National Park boasts a forest different from any other. The park was established in 1933 to protect an extraordinary and picturesque plant - the giant saguaro cactus of the Sonoran Desert. The Saguaro's white blossom, which appears April through June, is Arizona's state flower.

THE ARIZONA TRAIL

Seven of the trips described in this book utilize segments of the state-wide Arizona Trail (AZT): Trips 15, 18, 21, 22, 23, 24, and 30.

Beginning at the Arizona/Mexico border and ending at the Arizona/Utah border, the 800-mile Arizona Trail winds a north-south path across the state. The trail links old mining camps, beautiful lakes, Indian cliff dwellings and charming little communities like Patagonia and Summerhaven with some of the most beautiful "sky islands" in the southwest.

At time of printing, the Arizona Trail is still evolving. Some passages are not yet complete, while others are in the

Graceful soap tree yuccas stand silhouetted against an evening sky

process of being re-routed or changed. The vision of the trail is a non-motorized pathway - a wilderness experience, far from the sounds and sights of urban America. Information about the route of the AZT in this area may change after the book goes to print, a situation beyond the author's control.

For more information about the Arizona Trail, you can contact the Arizona Trail Association at P.O. Box 36736, Phoenix, AZ 85067. (602) 252-4794. www.aztrail.org.

HOW TO USE THIS GUIDE

All *GETTING THERE* directions are from Kartchner Caverns State Park. The mileage is the actual driving distance from the park.

Each trip has a quick reference symbol to let the reader know if the trail is accessible to hikers, bicycles, horses or wheelchairs. Trail use categories are also noted in bold letters in the text.

Each trail is rated as Easy, Moderate or Diffiicult. Degree of difficulty, of course, is a matter of opinion. In general, difficulty is rated according to steepness and length. Trail lengths vary from 0.3 of a mile roundtrip to 17.5 miles roundtrip.

LEAVE NO TRACE

Please leave Arizona's backcountry as beautiful and unspoiled as you find it. If you packed it in, then pack it out. If you have room in your pack, pick up trash left by others less enlightened. Tread lightly. Don't cut corners on switchbacks. Leave no trace, so that those following you will also have an enjoyable wilderness experience.

SAFETY

Most important to planning a safe trek is your own physical condition and acclimation to Arizona's high elevations and heat and your own good judgement when gauging terrain and weather conditions.

Equestrians need to make sure that your animals are well shod, in excellent physical condition, experienced at negotiating steep narrow trails, and accustomed to Arizona's heat and high elevations.

Heat is probably the greatest danger to hikers in Arizona, especially in the lower elevations. In Saguaro National

Park, temperatures can soar to 120 degrees Fahrenheit in the summer. Avoid these trails during the hottest months of the year, or travel in the early morning or early evening hours. Always wear a hat, long sleeves, long pants and carry sunscreen. Hydrate yourself before you start out, and carry plenty of electrolyte-replacement fluids such as Gatorade. *There are no sources of safe drinking water along any of these trails.*

Lightning is a danger during the summer monsoons. Plan your trips so that you are off mountain peaks and high, exposed ridgelines by noon, if hiking during the rainy season.

Rattlesnakes, in most cases, will not bite unless they feel threatened. They are earth tone colors: brown, black, tan, yellow and gray. In other words, they are well camouflaged. Don't sit down or step over or reach under rocks, logs or bushes without looking first.

Do you know what a rattlesnake sounds like? Unless you have heard the sound before, you might not recognize it. It is actually a buzzing rather than a rattle. A rattlesnake can sound like a locust buzzing in the leaves.

Although your chance of being bitten by a snake is remote, Arizona Poison Control recommends that trail users carry a good venom extractor, such as the Sawyer extractor, and know how to use it. These can be purchased at Wal-Mart or other outdoor or camping supply stores.

Death from a rattlesnake bite is very rare, so if you are bitten, don't panic. Don't run and don't attempt to kill the snake. Identifying the type of rattlesnake is not necessary, because hospitals use the same antivenin for all rattlesnake bites. Apply your extractor and walk to the nearest vehicle.

Illegal Immigrants. It is possible that you might encounter illegal immigrants from Mexico along some of these trails. For the most part these are ordinary people searching for a better life; however as with people everywhere, there may be the occasional "bad apple". We recommend that you don't hike alone and if you should see immigrants, do not approach them.

Plan ahead, be alert, watch and listen and enjoy the beautiful trails in and around Kartchner Caverns State Park.

View along the Guindani Trail

KARTCHNER CAVERNS STATE PARK
and the WHETSTONE MOUNTAINS

Officially opened in November 1999, Kartchner Caverns State Park (KCSP) encompasses 550 acres at the base of the Whetstone Mountains, southeast of Tucson. The caverns, the focus of the park, are concealed beneath one of the many small rocky hills that comprise the foothills of the Whetstones.

The caverns were discovered by caving enthusiasts Randy Tufts and Gary Tenen, in 1974. The two kept the cave a secret as they explored it over the next two years. In 1978 Tufts and Tenen told the property owners, the Kartchner family, about their discovery and in 1988, fourteen years after the cave was discovered, the property was purchased by Arizona State Parks.

Kartchner Caverns is a "living" cave with exquisite, world-class formations, including some that are quite rare. It is the goal of Arizona State Parks to protect the fragile environment of the caverns, and to that end they have installed air-lock doors and environmental stations within the cave to monitor temperature and humidity.

The Discovery Center is the best way to begin your visit to the caverns. The center offers a gift shop and bookstore, exhibits, and a large-screen amphitheater. Tours of the caverns, which leave from the Discovery Center, take about an hour and reservations are recommended. Other highlights of the park include a hummingbird garden, a picnic area and hiking and biking trails. The well-designed campground has hot showers and electric hookups.

The rugged Whetstone Mountains are a small range,

located within Coronado National Forest. The mountain range is thought to have earned its name because of a deposit of a hard, fine-grained rock once used to sharpen cutlery and tools.

Because much of the Whetstone range is bordered by private ranch land and state land which requires a permit from the Arizona State Land Department to cross, access to the Whetstones can be difficult and there are few trails. As a result, some areas are as wild and untouched now as they were in the mid-1800s, when Apache Indians sought refuge in the remote canyons.

Javelinas are common in the areas around Kartchner Caverns; however, like most wildlife, they are most safely viewed from a distance.

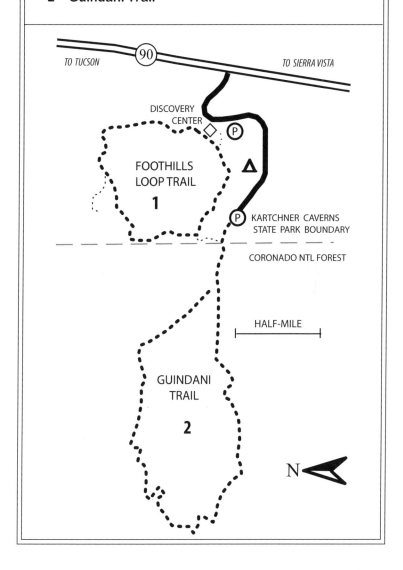

MAP 1
KARTCHNER CAVERNS STATE PARK
1 - Foothills Loop Trail
2 - Guindani Trail

TRIP 1

FOOTHILLS LOOP TRAIL

It's difficult to imagine that almost underfoot, there are enormous crystal-filled chambers. Beneath the rocks and cactus, tourists are enjoying a humid 68 degrees. Water is dripping from stalactite to stalagmite and an underground lake reflects the lights that have been placed to illuminate the formations and the pathways. After a visit to Kartchner Caverns, you may wonder how often you have walked over the top of hidden worlds.

Bicycles, horses and **pets** are not allowed on this trail. See the Guindani Trail for bicycles.

LOCATION: The trail is within Kartchner Caverns State Park. The trailhead is just outside of the Discovery Center, beyond the hummingbird garden.

There is an entrance fee per vehicle (up to four people) to enter the park. An additional fee is required to go on a cave tour and reservations are recommended.

LENGTH: 2.5-mile loop

RATING: Moderate

CONTACT AGENCY: Kartchner Caverns State Park
(520) 586-4100

TRAIL DESCRIPTION:

For visitors to Kartchner Caverns State Park, the Foothills Loop Trail offers an interesting contrast from the high humidity of the caverns to the spacious, arid climate of the Chihuahuan Desert.

The 2.5-mile Loop Trail leads from the park's Discovery Center to an oak and mesquite woodland along Guindani Wash. Several benches have been tucked into shady nooks, before the trail ventures out into the desert ecosystem of prickly pear cactus, ocotillo, sotol and mesquite. The route circles around the small hill above the caverns before climbing to a saddle and a conveniently placed bench for enjoying the views.

From the saddle, a side trail leads steeply for 0.4 miles to the summit of a hill, topped with a rock cairn. Views are impressive. To the northwest are the Rincon Mountains, just east of Tucson. Then, in a clockwise rotation, are the Winchesters, and the ragged pink pinnacles of the Dragoon Mountains, near Tombstone. The Mule Mountains of Bisbee, and San Jose Peak in Mexico are visible to the southeast. Due south the high peaks of the Huachucas mark the location of Sierra Vista, while the rugged Whetstone Mountains form the western horizon.

From the saddle it is an easy downhill walk, as the trail swings south and loops back to the Discovery Center.

TRIP 2

GUINDANI TRAIL

The Guindani Trail utilizes some scenic old roads in the foothills of the Whetstones, behind Kartchner Caverns State Park. The route winds through a pretty little canyon, then climbs a high saddle affording spacious views of the surrounding area. The trail is located on the National Forest, however the only way to access it is through the state park

Although the trail is open to **bicyclists***, it is very steep and rocky in places.* **Horses** *are not allowed within Kartchner Caverns State Park.*

LOCATION: The trailhead is located within Kartchner Caverns State Park. There is an entrance fee per vehicle (up to four people) to enter the park. An additional fee is required to go on a cave tour and reservations are recommended.

LENGTH: A 4.2-mile loop

RATING: Moderate. Some steep, rocky areas.

CONTACT AGENCY: Kartchner Caverns State Park
(520) 586-4100
Coronado National Forest, Sierra Vista Ranger District.
(520) 378-0311

Signs point the way on the Guindani Trail

GETTING THERE: From the park's main entrance, follow the road for 1.3 miles past the Discovery Center parking lots and the campground to a parking lot and restrooms on the left side of the road. This is the Guindani Trailhead.

TRAIL DESCRIPTION:

The trail leaves from the west side of the parking area and travels a short distance to a gate that marks the border between Kartchner Caverns State Park and Coronado National Forest. This is also the junction with a short path that connects to the Foothills Loop Trail, a 2.5-mile hiking trail within the park.

After passing through the gate, the trail heads directly west toward the Whetstone Mountains. Watch for rock cairns to direct you. At 0.4 miles from the parking area, the trail ends at a junction with two old dirt roads and a sign announcing the Guindani Trail.

Turn right following the old rocky roadbed as it winds northwest into the scenic, narrow canyon that becomes Guindani Wash. The route, which is lined with large white boulders, barrel cactus and yuccas, gradually gains in elevation as it swings west. Below in the wash, some good-size ash and oak trees are growing among small, seasonal pools of water.

A mile from the parking area, the route swings right and drops down into the wash, which may have running water and masses of blue morning glories, red penstemon and other wild flowers, following the summer rains.

Eventually the path leaves the creek, curving steeply up a hillside. It passes above the remnants of what appears, incredibly, to have been an old road, with boulders stacked high on each side. Traveling high above the creek, there are nice views of the little pools and waterfalls that ripple down through the boulders below.

The trail plays tag with the creek until it reaches a signed junction with the Cottonwood Saddle Trail #386. This trail travels north to Cottonwood Canyon and several 4WD roads, but there is no public access across private land. Take the left fork as the trail leaves the creek for the last time and climbs for another half mile to a gate and a high saddle.

At an elevation of 5,658 feet, the views of the Whetstone range and the surrounding area are spacious. From here it is all downhill, as the trail circles around the grassy south face and then the east face of the hill, affording a bird's eye view of Kartchner Cavern State Park below.

At length, the trail arrives at a wooden sign directing trail users toward the park. Half a mile farther is the unmarked junction of two old roads. Stay left and in a short distance another sign marks where the loop begins. Watch closely here for a rock cairn, marking where the trail leaves the road and travels back to the parking area.

An oasis in the desert: the San Pedro River

SAN PEDRO RIVER

The San Pedro Valley has been a haven for humans and wildlife since prehistoric times. Thirteen thousand years ago people from the Clovis culture hunted mammoths and other Ice Age animals in the area. Later, people from the Hohokam culture are believed to have left the petroglyphs that are found carved on rocks along the river.

The King of Spain established a fort along the banks of the San Pedro River in 1776. Disintegrating remains of the 200 year-old adobe walls are still visible, on a high bluff overlooking the river.

The river played an important part in the early mining ventures of the area. The ghost town of Fairbank is an excellent example of the mining towns that appeared along the river in the late 1800s. Mills were built that utilized water from the river for the process of extracting gold and silver.

The San Pedro Riparian National Conservation Area (SPRNCA) was designated by Congress on November 18, 1988, as the first globally important bird area in the United States. Managed by the Bureau of Land Management (BLM) the SPRNCA contains 58,000 acres of land along the San Pedro River, from the Mexico border to the small community of St. David, 10 miles south of I-10. The purpose of the designation was to protect this desert riparian ecosystem, a remnant of cottonwood/willow habitat that is becoming increasingly rare in other parts of the west.

The San Pedro River has been described as "a ribbon of green in a sea of brown." Riparian corridors provide extra cover, cooler, more humid conditions and more food than surrounding dry, upland habitats. The San Pedro is very important to migrating birds that breed in the north and winter in the south. The bird life attracts birdwatchers from all over the world. Between two to four million birds of over 250 species, migrate and winter along the river annually, while another 100 species are year-round inhabitants. Over 80 kinds of mammals, including recently re-introduced beavers and 40 species of reptiles and amphibians are found along the river.

The remains of adobe walls mark this ancient Spanish fort

TRIP 3

PRESIDIO SANTA CRUZ DE TERRENATE

This Spanish presidio, or fort, was established by an Irish mercenary for the King of Spain, in 1776. Terrenate is part of a once extensive network of fortresses that marked the northern extension of New Spain into the New World. The presidio was beset with problems from the start. Apache raids, insufficient supplies, low morale and isolation from other Spanish outposts all contributed to its demise. A report written in 1781 by the last commander of the presidio, described the incessant attacks by Apaches. After losing more than eighty men in less than five years, the fort was abandoned.

Two hundred years later, only a stone foundation and disintegrating adobe walls remain. The well-maintained trail has thoughtfully-placed benches for resting and admiring the view. The BLM has installed interpretive signs at this unique and fragile archeological site.

Bicycles, horses, and **leashed pets** *are allowed on the trail to the site, but NOT on the interpretive loop.*

DRIVING DISTANCE FROM KCSP: 20 miles

LOCATION: Iron Horse Ranch Road to a bluff overlooking the San Pedro River.

LENGTH: 2.5 miles roundtrip

RATING: Easy

CONTACT AGENCY: Bureau of Land Management (520) 439-6400

GETTING THERE: Passenger car. From KCSP drive south on Highway 90 for 10 miles to Highway 82. Turn left (east) on Highway 82 and drive 8 miles to Iron Horse Ranch Road (milepost 60). Turn left (north) on Iron Horse Ranch Road and drive 1.8 miles to the parking area on the right.

TRAIL DESCRIPTION:

From the parking area follow the trail east through a

MAP 2
SAN PEDRO RIVER
3 - Presidio Santa Cruz deTerrenate
4 - Fairbank River Loop Trail

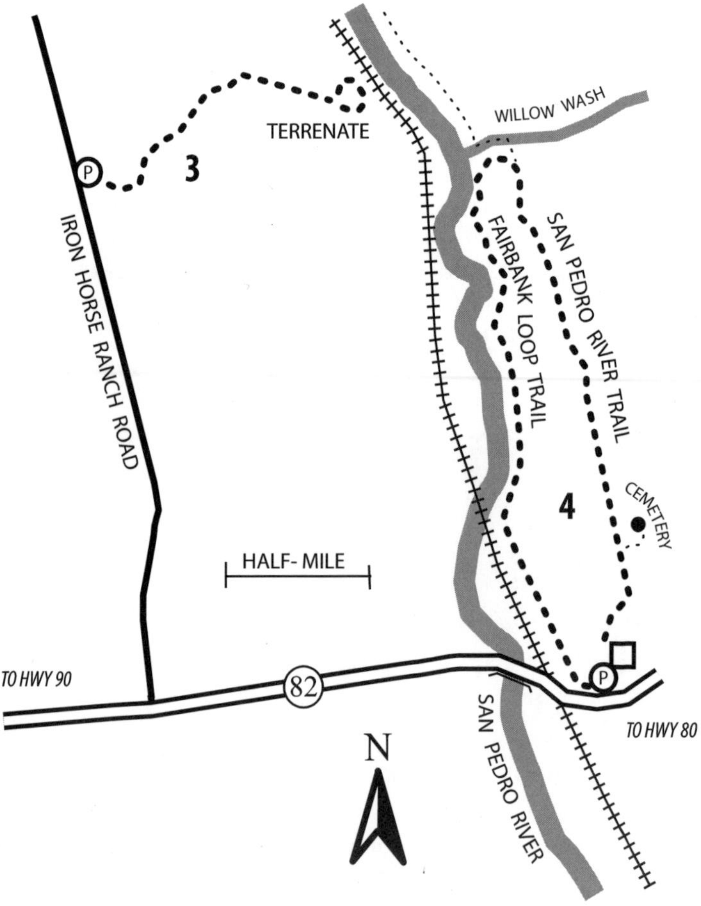

TERRENATE

WILLOW WASH

3

IRON HORSE RANCH ROAD

FAIRBANK LOOP TRAIL

SAN PEDRO RIVER TRAIL

4

CEMETERY

HALF- MILE

TO HWY 90

82

TO HWY 80

SAN PEDRO RIVER

N

gray-green landscape of scrubby, thorny, creosote, mesquite, and other small shrubs. Look for the long spines of the Crucifixion Thorn. This is an interesting plant that will not be seen in any other of our hikes. It is an easy, gradual downhill walk with frequent resting benches and nice views of the Dragoon Mountains to the east, and the cottonwoods along the San Pedro River.

At 0.7 miles the trail climbs up onto an abandoned railroad bed. Look back to admire the Whetstone Mountains to the west. Turn right and follow this elevated grade for 0.3 miles to the visitor registration box and restroom.

The interpretive loop is 0.5 miles in length. There are precautionary signs warning that the cliff overlooking the river is very steep and that there are no guardrails. A memorial plaque, placed by the Warrant Officers of Fort Huachuca, honors the Spanish soldiers who died here over two hundred years ago.

We don't recommend trying to hike to the river from here. The railroad tracks below the cliff are still in use, and both the rail-line and the river are a corridor for illegal immigrants travelling north from Mexico. Return the way that you came. Please stay on the trails and protect this historic site for future generations.

FAIRBANK RIVER LOOP TRAIL

Fairbank is a ghost town situated on the eastern bank of the San Pedro River. Once a thriving boomtown, Fairbank was established with the building of the railroad in 1881. It was the closest railroad stop to the bustling mining town of Tombstone.

Fairbank was built on an old Mexican land grant, the San Juan de las Boquillas y Nogales, which was purchased by the Boquillas Land and Cattle Company in 1901. The adobe Commercial Building, which once housed a general store and post office, was used into the 1970s.

The Bureau of Land Management acquired the property as part of the San Pedro Riparian National Conservation Area in 1986. Pamphlets available in the Commercial Building and interpretive signs with reproductions of old photographs tell the story of Fairbank. A self-guided tour of the buildings is available. Remember that it is illegal to remove any historic artifacts (including old bottles and cans, old metal or pottery) from public lands. Help to preserve our historic places.

The San Pedro Trail and the River Loop Trail are open to **bicyclists**, **equestrians**, *and* **leashed pets**, *as well as hikers, however the trail up to the cemetary is restricted to hikers only.*

Be aware that illegal immigrants from Mexico sometimes travel along the river, the railroad tracks and even the River Loop Trail.

DRIVING DISTANCE FROM KCSP: 20 miles

LOCATION: Fairbank at Highway 82 and the San Pedro River

LENGTH: 4-mile loop

RATING: Easy. This trail can be extremely hot in the spring and summer. Be prepared.

CONTACT AGENCY: Bureau of Land Management (520) 439-6400. Live-in Site Host (520) 457-3395.

GETTING THERE: Passenger Car. From KCSP drive south on Highway 90, ten miles to Highway 82. Turn left (east) on Highway 82 and drive ten miles to the San Pedro River bridge. After crossing the river bridge and then a railroad bridge, turn left into the Fairbank Townsite parking area. There is generally room in the back parking area for horse trailers. Large groups should call ahead.

TRAIL DESCRIPTION:
The San Pedro River Trail travels north from Fairbank along an old railroad grade. It is a pleasant, level walk through shady mesquite woodlands mixed with open grassy areas and fleeting views of the distant Cottonwood-lined river.

At 0.4 miles, watch for a path on the right, leading up a small hill to the Fairbank cemetery. The short climb is well worth the trip. There are over a hundred gravesites, some

The Fairbank cemetary   *Courtesy Debra Wright*

marked with stone mounds and weathered wooden crosses. The top of the hill provides an expansive view of the San Pedro Valley and the distant Whetstone Mountains. In late spring the air is fragrant with the blooms of mesquite and white-thorn acacia. Hikers may visit, but the path is not open to bicycles or horses.

Continuing along the San Pedro River Trail, watch for the foundations of the Grand Central Mill, built to process silver ore from the Tombstone mines. Except for the massive stone and cement wall to the right of the trail, little else remains.

0.4 miles beyond the millsite is a junction with the River

Loop Trail, which returns to Fairbank. According to signs, you may choose to continue beyond the loop trail junction, utilizing the San Pedro River Trail to access the ruins of a Spanish fort, Presidio Santa Cruz de Terrenate, on the other side of the river (see Trip 3). Or, you could continue north for 2 miles to the remains of another riverside mill camp known as Contention City. However, the trail is not maintained beyond this point, and as mentioned earlier, it is sometimes used by illegal immigrants.

To continue on the San Pedro River Trail, follow the route as it drops down to a wide, sandy arroyo, Willow Wash. Turn left and follow the wash 0.5 miles to the San Pedro's sandy bank. Be careful if wading in the river, because it is known to have areas of quicksand.

To return to Fairbank using the River Loop Trail, turn left at the junction. The River Loop Trail parallels the east bank of the San Pedro River for two miles, as it wanders between mesquite bosque and scenic cliff-edge views of the river. The trail is, at times, very close to the sometimes-undercut banks of the river. Hang on to small children and don't ride horses to cliff-edge. The loop trail eventually leaves the river to follow the railroad bed back to Highway 82 and the Fairbank parking lot.

The old schoolhouse stands empty at Fairbank

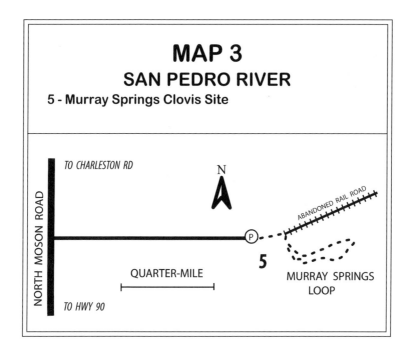

MAP 3
SAN PEDRO RIVER
5 - Murray Springs Clovis Site

TO CHARLESTON RD

N

NORTH MOSON ROAD

ABANDONED RAIL ROAD

P

5

QUARTER-MILE

MURRAY SPRINGS
LOOP

TO HWY 90

TRIP 5

MURRAY SPRINGS
CLOVIS SITE

This easy, barrier-free interpretive loop showcases one of the oldest archeological sites ever excavated in North America. Discovered in 1966, the site was excavated until 1971 with funding from the National Geographic Society and the National Science Foundation.

Archeologists from the University of Arizona uncovered the remains of several extinct animals including camels, bison and a mammoth nicknamed "Big Eloise". An ancient campsite, Clovis spear points and tools are evidence that humans hunted and butchered these huge Ice Age animals over 13,000 years ago.

The San Pedro Valley has more sites of this time period than anywhere else in the United States. The Clovis culture was named for the first such site found near Clovis, New Mexico in 1932.

Although this is designed as a barrier-free, **wheelchair** *accessible trail, summer floods sometimes damage the bridge. Call the BLM for an update on repairs.* **Bicycles** *and* **horses** *are not allowed on the interpretive loop. However, for those who wish to make a longer hike or ride,* **bicycles** *and* **horses** *are allowed on a trail that follows an abandoned railroad bed east for 2.3 miles to the San Pedro River. This trail is not maintained and may be badly overgrown or eroded in places.*

DRIVING DISTANCE FROM KCSP: 30 miles

LOCATION: West of the San Pedro River, on north Moson Road, between Charleston Road and Highway 90.

LENGTH: 0.6-mile interpretive loop

RATING: Easy. Barrier-free.

CONTACT AGENCY: Bureau of Land Management
(520) 458-3559

GETTING THERE: Passenger car. From KCSP drive south on highway 90 for 18.7 miles through Huachuca City, to the Highway 90 bypass, marked by a stoplight. Turn left, and travel 4 miles to a stoplight, and junction with Charleston Road. There is a shopping center on the left. Turn left on Charleston Road and drive 4.8 miles to Moson Road. Turn right on Moson Road and drive 1.8 miles, to a sign for Murray Spring Clovis Site. Turn left on a gravel road and drive 0.5 miles to the large parking area.

TRAIL DESCRIPTION:
Leaving the parking area, follow the wide, well-maintained trail east a short distance to a trail junction. Stay to the right, then follow the loop trail to the left. The trail travels above the curves of a deep wash, with views into the mammoth kill area, the bison kill area, and the campsite where a hearth and tools were found. Interpretive signs give a glimpse of life at the close of the Ice Age and tell of the historic excavations. The loop takes you full circle, and then return the way that you came.

TRIP 6

SAN PEDRO HOUSE
KINGFISHER POND LOOP

The San Pedro Riparian National Conservation Area, designated by Congress in 1988 as the first globally important bird area in the United States, is managed by the Bureau of Land Management.

The San Pedro House, operated by Friends of the San Pedro, is a historic ranch house that now serves as a bookstore and visitor information center. The house, built in the 1930s, was used by cowboys who worked for the Del Valle Ranch. The huge Fremont cottonwood tree west of the house is one of the largest in Arizona. The tree is believed to be 100 to 150 years old.

There are a number of loop trails that can be accessed from the San Pedro House visitor center. The area is very popular with birders. Ask about the recently reintroduced beavers. A beaver lodge may be visible along this hike.

Trails are open to hikers, **bicyclists, equestrians,** *and* **leashed pets;** *segments of the Kingfisher Pond Loop are accessible to* **wheelchairs.** *Camping permits are available and there is a resident site host.*

Trails are not named or numbered at time of printing, however information and trail maps are available at the San Pedro House. The trails offer the opportunity to observe and enjoy a lush and shady riparian desert ecosystem.

DRIVING DISTANCE FROM KCSP: 30 miles

LOCATION: San Pedro River east of Sierra Vista

LENGTH: 1.5 mile loop. There are other loop trails from the San Pedro House, that vary from 1 mile to 2.5 miles in length.

RATING: Easy. Portions are barrier-free.

CONTACT AGENCY: Bureau of Land Management
(520) 439-6400
Friends of the San Pedro River (520) 508-4445

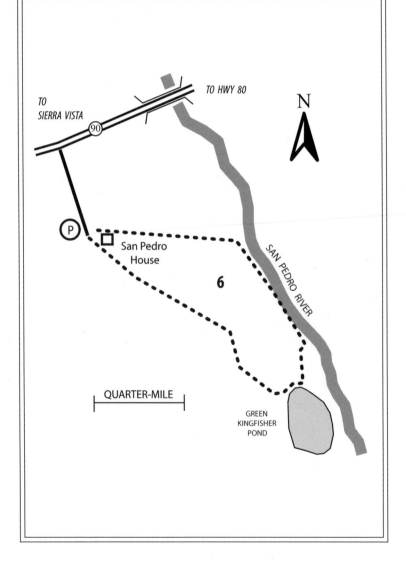

MAP 4
SAN PEDRO RIVER
6 - San Pedro House - Kingfisher pond Loop

TO HWY 80

TO
SIERRA VISTA

90

N

P

San Pedro
House

6

SAN PEDRO RIVER

QUARTER-MILE

GREEN
KINGFISHER
POND

GETTING THERE: Passenger car. From KCSP drive south on Highway 90 for 18.7 miles, passing through Huachuca City to the Highway 90 bypass, which is marked by a stoplight. Turn left, and travel 4.5 miles to Fry Boulevard (Highway 90/92 junction). Turn left (east) and follow Highway 90 for 7 miles. Watch for the entrance to the San Pedro House on the right, before the San Pedro River bridge.

TRAIL DESCRIPTION:

The wide, well-maintained trail leaves the San Pedro House traveling east toward the river, through an open area that was once an agricultural field. At 0.2 miles the path arrives at a bench, where it makes a sharp right turn. Continue east a few steps for a nice view of the river.

The route heads south as it parallels the river to another bench. Here it leaves the field, dropping down over the steep bank to the river below. The trail continues south beneath a lush overstory of cottonwood and willow trees. The river's serene, shaded banks attract a variety of birds and animals. A bench, placed in a lovely streamside setting, is perfect for viewing the river and watching for wildlife.

Before long the trail leaves the leafy oasis, curving out into an open field with nice views of the Huachuca Mountains on the western horizon.

The trail leads to Green Kingfisher Pond, named for the rare birds that sometimes nest here. Cattails, willows and small cottonwood trees rim the pond. This is a good place to observe great blue herons and other water fowl. Watch for the brilliant flash of vermillion flycatchers darting into the arching cottonwood canopy along the river.

At time of printing, the trail from the pond heading west was overgrown, with a large downed tree lying over the trail. Ducking under the tree, follow the trail as it connects with an abandoned road. Trail signs guide hikers along the edge of a field, through an area of grass and mesquite trees, to a junction. Turn left and follow the old road to the visitor center and a series of kiosks that explain the natural history and environmental importance of the San Pedro River.

Council Rocks are a favorite destination in the Dragoons

DRAGOON MOUNTAINS

The pink, wind-sculpted pinnacles of the Dragoon Mountains northeast of Tombstone mark the final resting place of the famous Apache leader, Cochise. In the mid 1800's, as a tide of settlers brought increasing conflict to their homeland, a group of Chiricahua Apaches, under Cochise, sought shelter in the canyons now known as Cochise Stronghold. The rocky fortress with its eerie wind-sculpted rocks and the thick oak, juniper and manzanita vegetation provided an ideal refuge, with rocky canyons that offered escape routes in several directions.

In 1861 Cochise was unjustly accused of kidnapping the son of a rancher and stealing some cattle. When Cochise denied the accusation, he and some of his family members were taken as prisoners. Although Cochise escaped, one of his men who tried to follow him was killed and the rest of his family captured. This incident resulted in full-scale warfare between the Apaches and Americans for the next ten years. Cochise was a master of guerilla warfare – a leader who was never conquered in battle.

By 1867 Tom Jeffords, a mail agent who employed riders to carry the mail between towns along the Rio Grande and Tucson, had lost 14 men to the Apaches. It is said that he boldly entered the Stronghold alone to meet with Cochise, and the two men became lifelong friends.

In 1872 Jeffords helped arrange a peace treaty with Cochise, and as part of the agreement, the traditional homeland of the Chiricahuas was designated as their reservation. Cochise remained free until his death in 1874, and according to legend is buried in a secret place somewhere in the Dragoon Mountains. Only two years after his death, the U.S. reneged on the agreement and abolished the reservation. The remaining Chiricahuas were sent north to the San Carlos Apache Reservation.

The name "Dragoon" means a heavily-armed, mounted trooper. The Dragoon Mountains were named for the 3rd U.S. Cavalry that was stationed near the area.

All of the trails described in this chapter are accessed from Forest Road 687, an especially scenic dirt road that winds around the west side of the Dragoons, through grasslands dotted with oaks and decorated with rock sculptures. F.R. 687 is popular with both equestrians and mountain bicyclists.

A fortress of balanced rocks and towering pinnacles

TRIP 7

SLAVIN GULCH

This hike follows an old road through a narrow canyon of impressive, salmon-colored granite cliffs and balanced rock formations. It's a steep climb through a riparian setting that harbors sparkling pools of water and waterfalls in the rainy months.

The route affords a good opportunity for viewing wildlife. Watch for small Coues white-tail deer and long-nosed coatimundis. Listen for the pretty song of the little canyon wren, a series of clear, descending notes, echoing from the rocky walls. The hike ends at the site of an abandoned lead and zinc mine, high on the side of the canyon.

Bicycles, horses, *and* **leashed pets** *are allowed on this trail, but it is steep, rocky and narrow in places and may require cutting back vegetation to get horses through. Experienced trail horses only.*

DRIVING DISTANCE FROM KCSP: 40 miles

LOCATION: Dragoon Mountains northeast of Tombstone.

LENGTH: 7.5 miles round trip

RATING: Difficult, with an elevation gain of 1400 feet

CONTACT AGENCY: Coronado National Forest, Douglas Ranger District (520) 364-3468

GETTING THERE: High-clearance vehicles recommended. From KCSP drive south on Highway 90 for ten miles to Highway 82. Turn left (east) on Highway 82 and drive sixteen miles to Highway 80. Turn right (south) on Highway 80 and drive 1.2 miles to Middlemarch Road. Turn left (east) onto graveled Middlemarch Road and drive 10 miles to FR 687. Turn left (north) on FR 687 and follow the winding dirt road for 2.8 miles. At this point the road turns sharply left, while straight ahead is a "road closed" sign and an earthen berm to prevent vehicle access. Park here.

TRAIL DESCRIPTION:

Follow the old road through rolling grassland dotted with oak trees, toward the wind-sculpted cliffs that are the distinguishing feature of the Dragoons. After a mile the road ends and a trail begins at the dramatic entrance to Slavin Gulch, which is formed by giant boulders that have tumbled down from above.

The rocky little path climbs up through boulders, beneath high cliff walls. The trail follows along the east wall of the canyon, and during the monsoon season the gulch holds pools of water. In the evening, the canyon echoes with frog songs.

As the trail climbs, oak, bear grass and sotol are replaced by pinyon pines and manzanita. Odd, sometimes bizarre rock formations along the trail invite your imagination to run wild. Soon, you can see the remains of mining equipment on a distant hillside.

3.5 miles from where you parked, the trail passes the remnants of a collapsed wooden structure on the left, and then the trail makes a sharp horseshoe turn to the right. There are beautiful views looking back down the canyon toward the southwest. 0.2 miles farther the trail arrives at an area littered with a tangle of old timbers and rusted metal - the decaying remains of an ore chute. Above, on the side of the mountain is the abandoned mine. The Forest Service cautions hikers not to enter the mine or climb on the old structures. Return the way that you came.

TRIP 8

COUNCIL ROCKS

This amazing jumble of giant granite boulders is said to be the place where Cochise, leader of the Chiricahua Apaches, met with Tom Jeffords and General O.O. Howard in 1872. Howard, sent by President Ulysses S. Grant to end the hostilities and negotiate for peace, had enlisted the help of Jeffords. The resulting, but short-lived treaty created a Chiricahua reservation of over 300 square miles in southeastern Arizona.

MAP 5
DRAGOON MOUNTAINS
7 - Slavin Gulch
8 - Council Rocks
9 - Cochise Trail - West Stronghold

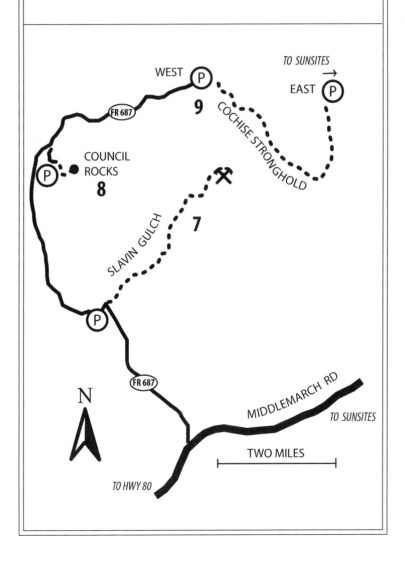

The extraordinary friendship between Cochise and Tom Jeffords inspired a best-selling novel, Blood Brother, in 1947, and later a movie version, Broken Arrow, starred Jeff Chandler as Cochise and Jimmy Stewart as Jeffords.

Council Rocks was an important meeting place for other Native Americans hundreds of years before the arrival of the Apaches. The setting is a gallery of rock art, with weathered and fragile pictographs in red and ocher, decorating the walls. These paintings are similar to designs used by prehistoric Mogollon people 1,000 years ago.

Don't touch the paintings. Council Rocks is a unique and special place - listed on the National Register of Historic Places. Please respect and protect it.

Bicycles *and* **horses** *are not allowed on this trail.*

DRIVING DISTANCE FROM KCSP: 44.2 miles

LOCATION: Dragoon Mountains northeast of Tombstone

LENGTH: 0.3 miles roundtrip

RATING: Moderate – very short but steep

CONTACT AGENCY: Coronado National Forest, Douglas Ranger District, (520) 364-3468

GETTING THERE: High-clearance vehicles recommended. From KCSP drive south on Highway 90 for ten miles to Highway 82. Turn left (east) on Highway 82 and drive sixteen miles to Highway 80. Turn right (south) on Highway 80 and drive 1.2 miles to Middlemarch Road. Turn left (east) onto graveled Middlemarch Road and drive 10 miles to FR 687. Turn left (north) on FR 687 and follow the winding dirt road for 6.7 miles, watching closely for a right turn onto FR 687K. The sign is behind a tree and difficult to see. Follow 687K for 0.3 miles to the parking area.

TRAIL DESCRIPTION:

The trail leaves the parking area on the east, through a fence with a gate. In summer the trail is lined with morning glories, coral bean plants and other wild flowers.

Almost immediately the trail starts to climb steeply up through a boulder-strewn drainage. Look for steps that are cut into the rocks. As the trail passes under a huge, overhanging boulder, look up. The largest wall of rock paintings is right over your head. Just beyond is an interpretive sign that describes the history of the area.

Wander through the mysterious jumble of enormous boulders that have toppled one upon another. Look for the mortars, or cylindrical holes in the rocks, where Indian women once sat, grinding nuts and seeds, and explore the hidden pathways and chambers that must have offered shelter to many who passed this way. Return the way that you came.

TRIP 9

COCHISE TRAIL # 279
West Stronghold

This scenic trail, which links two deep and rocky canyons, is a route once used by the Chiricahua Apaches. Cochise Stronghold lies in the heart of the Dragoon Mountains, an extensive maze of picturesquely eroded balanced rocks and spires. A natural fortress, sentinels on watch from its towering pinnacles could spot the approach of enemies on the flatlands below.

Trail # 279 travels from the West Stronghold trailhead to the developed campground in the East Stronghold, in a distance of only 4.75 miles. In contrast, the shortest distance driving from the west to the east stronghold would be over 50 miles of dirt road, or longer if paved roads are utilized!

The shady parking area is adjacent to a small seasonal creek. The fence has a pass-through for hikers to access the trail.

Bicycles *are allowed on this trail, but they must be lifted over the fence, and the trail is very steep and rocky.*

Equestrians *follow the fence line to the right. A faint trail cuts up the hill, bypassing the gate. There is room in the small parking area to turn a two-horse trailer, however equestrians may prefer the eastern approach, through Sunsites, which offers better roads and an equestrian staging area.*

The Dragoons offer scenic trails steeped in history

DRIVING DISTANCE FROM KCSP: 47 miles

LOCATION: Dragoon Mountains northeast of Tombstone

LENGTH: 1.7 miles one way to the Stronghold Divide. 4.7 miles one way, from the West Stronghold to the East Stronghold campground.

RATING: Moderate

CONTACT AGENCY: Coronado National Forest, Douglas Ranger District (520) 364-3468

GETTING THERE: A high-clearance vehicle is required. The road becomes very rocky and deeply rutted in places. From KCSP drive south on Highway 90 for ten miles to Highway 82. Turn left (east) on Highway 82 and drive sixteen miles to Highway 80. Turn right (south) on Highway 80 and drive 1.2 miles to Middlemarch Road. Turn left (east) onto graveled Middlemarch Road and drive 10 miles to FR 687. Turn left (north) on FR 687 and follow the winding dirt road for 10.4 miles to the trailhead at the end of the road.

TRAIL DESCRIPTION:

The well-maintained trail travels through oak, juniper, then manzanita and pinyon pines, as it climbs into the stronghold. The route travels on the south side of the canyon, with sweeping views into the drainage below. As the trail climbs, the canyon deepens. After a mile the trail narrows with steep switchbacks.

At 1.7 miles you reach a gate on a high, windswept saddle, that is the Stronghold Divide. From here you have great views into both the east and the west canyons. Return the way that you came, or continue for 3 miles to the East Stronghold campground and parking lot.

If you choose to continue down the trail to the east, there are some nice views, beautifully framed by the pink, wind-sculpted rocks. It is 1 mile to Half Moon Tank, a small pond that is rimmed with cattails and cottonwood trees, and then 2 more miles through an area of very scenic sculpted rocks to the sycamore and walnut trees that mark the east stronghold.

Carr Falls, after a summer thunderstorm

HUACHUCA MOUNTAINS

The Huachuca Mountains (pronounced Whachooka) are an excellent example of a southwestern "sky island". These beautiful mountains rise from the surrounding grasslands of the Chihuahuan Desert to the towering heights of the Canadian life zone, represented by 9,466 foot Miller Peak. The upper reaches of the mountains are usually snow-capped in the winter months.

Ramsey Canyon Preserve, owned and operated by the Nature Conservancy, is tucked into a canyon on the east side of the range. The conservancy, which operates a visitor center and a book store, offers information about some of the rare plants and animals that are found in the Huachucas.

While the northern portion of the range is part of Fort Huachuca's military base, and the southern end of the range is within Coronado National Memorial, the majority of the mountain range is within the Coronado National Forest, overseen by the Sierra Vista Ranger District. The Miller Peak Wilderness was established in 1984.

The Huachucas have a mining history dating back to the Spanish who mined silver for the kings of Spain. In the late 1800s and early 1900s small communities, such as Hamburg in Ramsey Canyon and Reef Townsite in Carr Canyon, evolved to support the mining and lumbering activities.

Fort Huachuca was established as a U.S. Army outpost in 1877 to protect settlers from Apache Indians. The Buffalo Soldiers, famed black cavalry and infantry troops, played an important part in the history of Fort Huacuca. Still an active military base today, Fort Huachuca's big, white, aerostat radar system balloon is usually visible, floating above the highest peaks of the Huachuca Mountains.

Many of the trails described in this chapter are linked, affording the opportunity for loop hikes. The state-wide

Arizona Trail (Crest Trail 103) can be accessed from both the Miller Canyon Trail and the Carr Peak Trail.

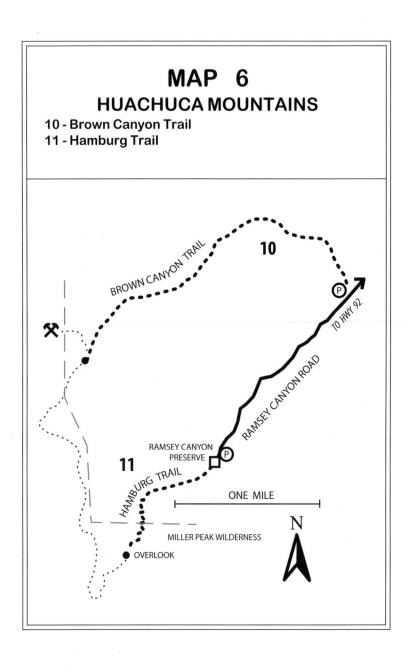

MAP 6
HUACHUCA MOUNTAINS
10 - Brown Canyon Trail
11 - Hamburg Trail

TRIP 10

BROWN CANYON TRAIL

Brown Canyon Trail begins in an area of rolling grass-covered hills, dotted with oak and manzanita, as it follows an abandoned dirt road for the first 2.5 miles. The route passes by an old gravesite and the ruins of a homestead, before entering a riparian canyon, leading to a shady grotto and a small waterfall and pool.

Brown Canyon Trail is sometimes used by hikers to connect with the Hamburg Trail, to make an 8-mile loop. Hikers can follow the Hamburg Trail through the Ramsey Canyon Preserve and then walk 1.5 miles down Ramsey Canyon Road, back to Brown Canyon.

Brown Canyon is popular with equestrians, and mountain bicyclists, however **bicycles** *may not continue into the Miller Peak Wilderness area and* **horses, bicycles,** *and* **pets** *are not allowed within the Ramsey Canyon Preserve.*

DRIVING DISTANCE FROM KCSP: 31 miles

LOCATION: Huachuca Mountain foothills.

LENGTH: 4.8 miles round-trip from Ramsey Canyon Road to the spring and back.

RATING: Easy to moderate.

CONTACT AGENCY: Coronado National Forest, Sierra Vista Ranger District. (520) 378-0311

GETTING THERE: Passenger car. From KCSP drive south on Highway 90, for 18.7 miles through Huachuca City, to the 90 bypass, marked by a stoplight. Turn left, and travel 4.5 miles to Fry Boulevard (Highway 90/92 junction). Here, Highway 90 turns left (east). Continue straight across the intersection (south) on Highway 92 for 6 miles and turn right (west) on Ramsey Canyon Road, traveling 2.1 miles to an unmarked Forest Service gate on the right. Pull through the gate and park.

TRAIL DESCRIPTION:

Follow the old road as it heads north, over a saddle into Brown Canyon. From the ridge, the route bears left or west as it descends to canyon bottom. The road crosses several washes and climbs a hillside. Hikers will pass an old cemetery and the ruins of an old homestead. In a little over 2 miles, a road junction is reached. The steep road to the right climbs for 1.5 miles to the abandoned Pomona Mine, where tungsten was mined in the 1930s.

Passing the junction, continue a short distance to a cement stock tank. The road ends here and the route continues as a trail, travelling up the shady canyon, to a stone-encased spring box.

For an interesting side trip that involves some off-trail rock-hopping, continue a short distance up-canyon, climbing toward layers of rock that are oddly bent and twisted. The beautiful little pool and waterfall are well worth the scramble. Return the way that you came.

For those who wish to continue on into Ramsey Canyon, or make an 8-mile loop, follow the trail as it leaves the canyon bottom to the left. A series of steep switchbacks lead to a saddle on the pine and oak-covered ridgeline that separates Brown and Ramsey Canyons.

Brown Canyon's accessibility contributes to the trail's popularity.
Courtesy Dawn-to-Dust Mountain Bike Club of Arizona

TRIP 11

RAMSEY CANYON PRESERVE
HAMBURG TRAIL

Ramsey Canyon Preserve, owned and operated by the Nature Conservancy, is renowned for its scenic beauty and abundant wildlife. In 1965 the site was designated as the first National Natural Landmark under the Historic Sites Act.

The preserve is home to some extremely rare plants and animals and up to 14 species of hummingbirds. In addition to great hiking and wildlife watching, the Nature Conservancy offers a visitor center, a gift shop and hummingbird garden, all of which are accessible to **wheelchairs***. Guided tours are available. The Preserve also operates a Bed and Breakfast.*

Parking is limited to 23 spaces, on a first come basis. The preserve is open 8:00 - 5:00 March 1st through October 31st, and 9:00 - 5:00 in the winter months. It is closed on Thanksgiving, Christmas and New Years Day. There is a nominal entrance fee.

Bicycles, horses *and* **pets** *are not permitted on trails within the preserve.*

DRIVING DISTANCE FROM KCSP: 33 miles

LOCATION: Ramsey Canyon Preserve/Coronado National Forest

LENGTH: 2 miles roundtrip

RATING: Difficult, with an elevation gain of over 1000 feet in 1 mile.

CONTACT AGENCY: Ramsey Canyon Preserve (520) 378-2785. Bed and Breakfast (520) 378-3010. Coronado National Forest (520) 378-0311

GETTING THERE: Passenger car. From KCSP drive south on Highway 90 for 18.7 miles, through Huachuca City, to the 90 bypass, which is marked by a stoplight. Turn left, and travel 4.5 miles to Fry Boulevard (Highway 90/92 junction). Here, Highway 90 turns left (east). Continue straight across the intersection (south) on Highway 92 for six miles and turn right (west) on Ramsey Canyon Road. Drive 4 miles to the preserve.

TRAIL DESCRIPTION:

The Hamburg Trail parallels Ramsey Creek through the preserve, past some historic log cabins. The route is shady beneath a canopy of enormous sycamores, Arizona oaks, ash, and big tooth maple trees that line the trail. Thoughtfully-placed benches are found along the well-maintained trail, all the way to the preserve/wilderness boundary.

Watch for the frequently-seen Coues whitetails, the second smallest deer in the United States. Visitors often see Painted Redstarts, wild turkeys, and a family of coatimundis that live in the canyon.

0.3 miles up the trail, an old cement pond holds one of the rarest amphibians in North America. The Ramsey Canyon Leopard Frog, a unique species that vocalizes under water, is found only in Ramsey Canyon and a few other sites within the Huachuca Mountains.

The route eventually leaves the old roadbed to climb in steep switchbacks and at 0.8 miles it reaches the boundary of the Miller Peak Wilderness. It is another 0.2 miles to the overlook, a rocky prominence that affords dramatic and sweeping views of upper Ramsey Canyon.

Return the way that you came, or for a longer loop hike, follow the Hamburg Trail for a half-mile, as it drops down to the canyon bottom and a junction with the Brown Canyon Trail. Follow the Brown Canyon Trail for 5 miles to Ramsey Canyon Road. Hike up Ramsey Canyon Road for 1.5 miles to the visitor center, for a total distance of 8 miles.

The Huachuca Mountains are home to wild Merriam turkeys

TRIP 12

PERIMETER TRAIL
Carr Canyon to Miller Canyon

The Perimeter Trail is the result of local community interest in having a lower elevation trail for hikers, **equestrians** *and mountain* **bicyclists***. The project has a long-range plan for 25-plus miles of trail. Traveling through the eastern foothills of the Huachuca Mountains, the trail will link the city of Sierra Vista with Coronado National Memorial. The Forest Service, in a cooperative effort with several community partners, is pursuing grants to complete the trail.*

A one-way hike can be made from Carr Canyon to Miller Canyon, by first leaving a vehicle at the Miller Canyon parking area. An 8.5-mile loop may also be done, by utilizing the Clark Spring/John Cooper trails, which are also described in this book. Leashed **dogs** *are allowed.*

DRIVING DISTANCE FROM KCSP: 32 miles

LOCATION: Trailheads on Carr Canyon Road and Miller

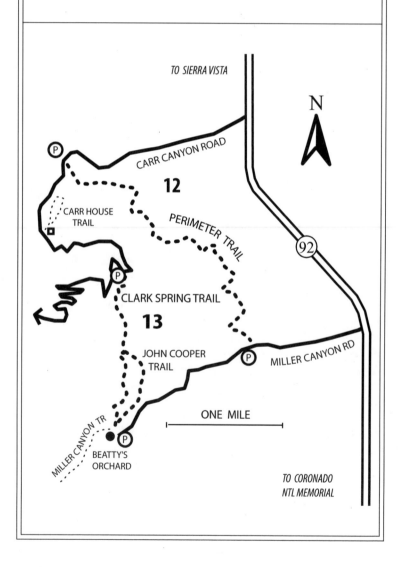

MAP 7
HUACHUCA MOUNTAINS
12 - Perimeter Trail
13 - Clark Spring / John Cooper Trails

TO SIERRA VISTA

N

P

CARR CANYON ROAD

12

CARR HOUSE
TRAIL

PERIMETER TRAIL

92

P

CLARK SPRING TRAIL

13

JOHN COOPER
TRAIL

P   MILLER CANYON RD

ONE MILE

MILLER CANYON TR

P

BEATTY'S
ORCHARD

TO CORONADO
NTL MEMORIAL

Canyon Road, south of Sierra Vista.

LENGTH: 3.7 miles one-way from Carr to Miller Canyon Road.

RATING: Easy

CONTACT AGENCY: Coronado National Forest, Sierra Vista Ranger District. (520) 378-0311

GETTING THERE: Passenger car. From KCSP drive south on Highway 90 for 18.7 miles, passing through Huachuca City to the 90 bypass, which is marked by a stoplight. Turn left, and travel 4.5 miles to Fry Boulevard (Highway 90/92 junction). Here, Highway 90 turns left (east). Continue straight across the intersection (south) on Highway 92 for 7 miles to Carr Canyon Road.

Turn right (west) on Carr Canyon Road. Travel 1.7 miles to the trailhead and parking areas on both sides of the road. There is a restroom on the right and a spacious pull-through parking area on the left side of the road that is large enough to accommodate a 4-horse trailer.

TRAIL DESCRIPTION:

The trail leaves the parking area on Carr Canyon Road heading southeast. Crossing a small creek bed, the path enters a wooded area of oak and juniper trees, and red-skinned manzanita bushes. There are nice views of the granite cliffs in upper Carr Canyon.

It is an easy uphill as the trail curves east, travelling above the Carr Canyon Road. At 1.8 miles the trail crosses a usually-dry, sandy creek bed. As it winds around the eastern foothills of the Huachucas, in and out of drainages, there are far-reaching views of the Hereford area, and the San Pedro Valley.

There is a gate (please close it) 2.3 miles from the trailhead and a view of Hereford Road, stretching east toward the distant Mule Mountains. O.7 miles later the path tops a rise with a view down into Miller Canyon. Stay with the trail as it curves to the right and descends toward the road. Two big rock cairns direct you south, across an abandoned road and into a pretty little grassy wash lined with sycamore trees.

At 3.7 miles this segment of the Perimeter Trail ends at the parking area on Miller Canyon Road. Pick up your vehicle if you have left one, or return the way that you came.

For an 8.3-mile loop turn right and continue up Miller Canyon Road for 1.3 miles, to the end of the road. Follow the Miller Canyon Trail a short distance to access the Clark Spring /John Cooper (mountain bike) trails.

TRIP 13

CLARK SPRING/JOHN COOPER TRAILS
Miller Canyon to Carr Canyon

Clark Spring Trail traverses the eastern slope of the Huachuca Mountains from upper Miller Canyon Road to Carr Canyon Road. Although it is two miles shorter than the Perimeter Trail, which also connects the two canyons lower down on the mountain, the Clark Spring Trail is rougher. It is a bit rockier with steeper climbs, and one very bad spot for horses. Clark Spring is usually dry and difficult to find. The Forest Service asks that you stay on the trail and carry plenty of drinking water.

The Clark Spring Trail has its charms, however, and it is also the access route for the John Cooper Bicycle Loop trail, which bypasses the Miller Peak Wilderness boundary and some of the rougher sections of the Clark Spring Trail. Equestrians and hikers may also use the John Cooper Trail.

An 8.5-mile loop can be made by utilizing the Perimeter Trail, which is also described in this book.

*Both routes are open to **bicycles** and **horses**. Leashed **dogs** are allowed.*

DRIVING DISTANCE FROM KCSP: 34.5 miles

LOCATION: Trailheads on Miller Canyon Road and Carr Canyon Road south of Sierra Vista.

LENGTH: 1.7 miles one-way from Miller Canyon Road to

Carr Canyon Road.

RATING: Moderate to difficult. This trail is steeper than the Perimeter Trail.

CONTACT AGENCY: Coronado National Forest, Sierra Vista Ranger District. (520) 378-0311

GETTING THERE: Passenger car. From KCSP drive south on Highway 90, for 18.7 miles through Huachuca City, to the 90 bypass, marked by a stoplight. Turn left, and travel 4.5 miles to Fry Boulevard (Highway 90/92 junction). Here, Highway 90 turns left (east). Continue straight across the intersection (south) on Highway 92 for 8.9 miles to Miller Canyon Road. Turn right (west) on Miller Canyon Road, traveling 2.5 miles to the trailhead at the end of the road.

TRAIL DESCRIPTION:

Leaving the north side of the parking area, follow the Miller Canyon Trail #106 a very short distance (0.1 miles) to a trail junction with Clark Spring Trail #124. This first part is very steep and rocky for bikes, but doesn't last long. Turn right on Clark Spring Trail, as it winds through a wooded landscape of manzanita, oak and pine, beneath a towering granite cliff. (To continue up the Miller Canyon Trail see Trip 15).

Just 0.2 miles from the parking lot is a sign for the Miller Peak Wilderness boundary, and a junction with the John Cooper Bicycle Trail. The bicycle trail forks to the right and then travels below, rejoining the Clark Spring Trail, 0.7 miles later. Hikers and equestrians may opt to go this way.

Continuing on the Clark Spring Trail, the route climbs steeply, coming to a place in the trail that is washed out with slick, tilted rocks. Because of the steep terrain here, getting around this section of trail with a horse is not only difficult, but potentially dangerous. It shouldn't pose a problem for hikers.

One half mile from the parking area watch for an interesting variety of yucca, on the right side of the trail. The banana yucca has large, 5-inch long fruit in late July and August that resemble a cluster of green bananas.

As the trail winds around the mountain, there are nice views to the east of the San Pedro Valley and the Mule

Mountains near Bisbee. There are occasional glimpses of the bicycle trail below. The route becomes soft and sandy, shaded by large junipers, pines and oaks.

0.9 miles into the hike the bicycle trail rejoins Clark Spring Trail, and soon after, the trail crosses a shady drainage with large trees. The route continues northwest through an opening in a fence line, traversing a rocky area that appears to be a long-abandoned and overgrown road. It is a half-mile farther to the Carr Canyon Road.

The trailhead, which is 3.5 miles up Carr Canyon Road from the highway, is easy to miss from the road. There is no noticeable parking area, and the sign is set back off the road. From here you can pick up your vehicle if you have left one, return the way that you came, or make an 8.5-mile loop by traveling down Carr Canyon Road for 1.6 miles to the Perimeter Trail, and back to Miller Canyon.

Huachuca peaks are blanketed in snow most winters

TRIP 14

CARR PEAK TRAIL

Carr Canyon offers the only developed campgrounds in the area, other than the one at KCSP. Located high on the east side of the Huachucas, the campgrounds (which have no dependable water source) are at the end of a narrow dirt road. It is a scenic drive as Carr Canyon Road makes a steep, switchback ascent from Highway 92 to the pine forests atop the mountain.

On the way, the road passes the Carr House Visitor Center (see map 7), which is open on weekends. The center has a delightful 0.7 mile loop trail that takes hikers by the impressive stone ruins of one of Carr Canyon's earliest homesteaders. The trail also affords a wonderful view of Carr Falls, a spectacular waterfall during the summer rains.

Carr Canyon Road may be closed with ice and snow in the winter months. The road is steep, rocky and narrow, with occasional wide spots for passing. It can be driven, with great care, in a passenger car, but high clearance is preferable.

The first trailhead to Carr Peak is located on the left side of the road, across from the Reef Townsite Campground. Reef Townsite was a small mining town in the early 1900s. There is a nice 0.7-mile interpretive loop trail that leaves from the back of the campground. The trail offers a stroll through a shady forest, where interpretive signs and old photographs describe the mining and geologic history of the area. The path passes the ruins of one of the mills and provides scenic vistas of the great, slanted rock formation that gave the Reef its name.

Equestrians: *The road is extremely steep and rough for horsetrailers. Those who decide to brave the road may want to proceed to the trailhead at the second campground, Ramsey Vista, 1.5 miles farther down the road. There are four tiny corrals and an area for parking horsetrailers. Leashed **dogs** are permitted. Because this trail enters the Miller Peak wilderness, **bicycles** are not allowed.*

DRIVING DISTANCE FROM KCSP: 37 miles

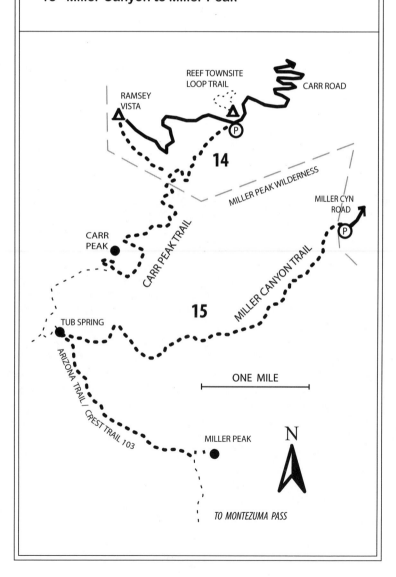

MAP 8
HUACHUCA MOUNTAINS
14 - Carr Peak Trail
15 - Miller Canyon to Miller Peak

REEF TOWNSITE
LOOP TRAIL

CARR ROAD

RAMSEY
VISTA

P

14

MILLER PEAK WILDERNESS

MILLER CYN
ROAD

CARR
PEAK

P

CARR PEAK TRAIL

MILLER CANYON TRAIL

15

TUB SPRING

ONE MILE

ARIZONA TRAIL / CREST TRAIL 103

MILLER PEAK

N

TO MONTEZUMA PASS

LOCATION: Huachuca Mountains. The trail travels from either campground to Carr Peak, within the Miller Peak Wilderness.

LENGTH: 5.5-miles roundtrip

RATING: Difficult. An elevation gain of over 1,800 feet.

CONTACT AGENCY: Coronado National Forest, Sierra Vista Ranger District. (520) 378-0311

GETTING THERE: Passenger car is possible, but a high-clearance vehicle is preferred. From KCSP drive south on Highway 90 for 18.7 miles, through Huachuca City, to the 90 bypass, which is marked by a stoplight. Turn left, and travel 4.5 miles to Fry Boulevard (Highway 90/92 junction). Here, Highway 90 turns left (east). Continue straight across the intersection (south) on Highway 92 for 7 miles to Carr Canyon Road. Turn right (west) on Carr Canyon Road. At 1.7 miles you will pass the parking area for the Perimeter Trail (Trip 12). It is 6.8 miles to the Reef Townsite campground and trailhead. This road may be icy or blocked with snow in the winter.

TRAIL DESCRIPTION:
The first part of the trek from the Reef Townsite trailhead follows a steep, rocky abandoned roadbed, heading directly toward Carr Peak. Soon the route enters a burned area, where ghost trees from the forest fire of 1977 still stand. Amongst the bleached white trunks of dead trees are small Gambel oaks, manzanitas, and some young conifer trees. Life has returned in the form of meadow grasses sprinkled with wild flowers.

It is just over half a mile to the junction with the Carr Peak Trail coming in from Ramsey Vista Campground. Turn left and follow this steep, scenic mountainside trail as it travels through groves of young aspen trees and grassy areas dotted with wildflowers in the summer. The trail affords expansive views into Miller Canyon, and you may see colorful hang gliders drifting on the air currents. As the trail climbs, there is evidence of the March 2002 Oversite Fire.

2.3 miles from the trailhead, in an area of charred trees, is a junction with the trail to the 9,200-foot summit of Carr

Enjoying the view from Carr Peak

Peak. The trail we have been following continues on for another mile to the Crest Trail, now part of the state-wide Arizona Trail.

Turn right onto the 0.3 miles trail to Carr Peak. The route switchbacks up through large Douglas firs, then winds through a jumble of white boulders to the bald summit of Carr Peak.

The peak affords magnificent 360° views of the vast southeastern Arizona landscape. Looking north, follow the jagged backbone of the Huachuca Mountains as it descends into the Babocomari drainage. Just north, paralleling Highway 90 are the Whetstone Mountains, home of Kartchner Caverns State Park. Beyond the Whetstones are the distant Rincon Mountains, and farther still, the Santa Catalinas east of Tucson.

To the east, the San Pedro River is marked by a thread of green vegetation. Across the valley rise the pink granite spires of the Dragoon Mountains east of Tombstone. Between the Dragoons, and the Mule Mountains of Bisbee to the southeast, lie the distant Chiricahua Mountains and Dos Cabezas.

Farther south stands solitary San Jose Peak in Sonora Mexico. Beyond, on the horizon, lie the Sierra Madre Mountains. The southern view is interrupted by the mass of Miller Peak, the highest peak in the Huachucas. The Patagonia Mountains and the Santa Rita Mountains are visible to the west. Return the way that you came, or continue on to Tub Spring and junctions with Miller Canyon Trail and the Crest Trail (Arizona Trail).

TRIP 15

MILLER CANYON TRAIL
to MILLER PEAK

9,466 foot Miller Peak is the highest point in the Huachuca Mountains and the highest point described in this book. The Miller Canyon Trail connects to the Crest Trail, (part of the state-wide Arizona Trail), as do many other trails in the Huachucas. With advance planning a vehicle could be left at another trailhead for the return trip.

Just beyond the parking area is the entrance to Beatty's Guest Ranch & Orchard, where apples are available from August through October, and honey and cold drinks are sold in the small gift shop year round. A favorite with birders, the Beattys offer rental apartments and cabins, tent camping and a public area to view hummingbirds.

Miller Canyon Trail is open to **horses***, however since it enters a wilderness area,* **bicycles** *are prohibited. Leashed* **dogs** *are allowed.*

DRIVING DISTANCE FROM KCSP: 34.6 miles

LOCATION: Huachuca Mountains. From the end of Miller Canyon Road to the summit of Miller Peak, within the Miller Peak Wilderness.

LENGTH: 11 miles round trip

RATING: Difficult. A steep climb with an elevation gain of almost 3,700 feet.

CONTACT AGENCY: Coronado National Forest, Sierra Vista Ranger District. (520) 378-0311
Beatty's Guest Ranch & Orchard. (520) 378-2728

GETTING THERE: Passenger car. From KCSP drive south on Highway 90 for 18.7 miles, through Huachuca City, to the 90 bypass, which is marked by a stoplight. Turn left, and travel 4.5 miles to Fry Boulevard (Highway 90/92 junction). Here, Highway 90 turns left (east). Continue straight across the intersection (south) on Highway 92 for 8.9 miles to Miller Canyon Road. Turn right (west) on Miller Canyon Road, traveling 2.5 miles to the trailhead at the end of the road.

TRAIL DESCRIPTION:

Leaving the north side of the parking area, follow the trail a short distance to a junction with the Clark Spring Trail, and stay left. The Miller Canyon Trail climbs around and above Beatty's orchard, then follows an old roadbed that travels above Miller Creek. At a fork in the road, stay right. At the junction with Hunter Canyon Trail, stay right.

This is one of the prettiest places in the Huchucas in late fall when the bigtooth maple trees are wearing their bright fall colors. After 1.5 miles the trail leaves the roadbed on the right, making a steep climb up the mountainside, shaded by tall ponderosa and white pines and ancient Douglas firs. Mine tunnels and the rusty remains of mining equipment attest to the active mining history of the area. Patches of scorched trees are evidence of the Oversite Fire of March 2002. In the last quarter-mile to the Crest Trail, the route passes through some larger burn areas.

3.5 miles from the parking area, the Crest Trail (part of the state-wide Arizona Trail) is reached. You are in the evergreen and aspen forest of the high country now, at an elevation of over 8,500 feet. Just to the left is Bathtub Spring, a usually reliable water source for wildlife. Max Baumkirchner, a miner who built a cabin in the area, had the old cast iron tub brought up by mules in the early 1800s. Bathtub Spring is an inviting place to take a break. The pleasant, shady saddle often rings with the songs of higher elevation birds that won't be seen in the flatlands below.

From the Miller Canyon Trail junction, follow the Crest/Arizona Trail to the left (south) for 1.5 miles to the signed trail to Miller Peak. From this junction, The Arizona Trail continues south for another 6.3 miles to Montezuma Pass, or 8 miles to the United States/Mexico border (See Trip 18). Turn left for Miller Peak. The half-mile climb through ponderosa pine trees and aspens brings you to the dramatic summit of Miller Peak and a 360-degree view of the world below.

To the southeast, a line of green vegetation marks the

Bathtub Spring, a junction of trails

San Pedro River. This is thought to have been the route of Francisco Vasquez de Coronado when he began his exploration of what is now the United States, over four hundred and fifty years ago. Pyramid-shaped San Jose Peak is visible just across the border in Sonora Mexico, and on the distant horizon are the Sierra Madre Mountains.

To the east, beyond the river are the Mule Mountains, and Bisbee, "Queen of the Copper Camps". Farther east lie the Chiricahua Mountains and Apache Pass. The classic western movie Stagecoach, starring John Wayne, was based on the battles between the U.S. Cavalry and the Apache Indians that took place there.

To the Northeast, the ragged pink cliffs of the Dragoon Mountains mark the final resting-place of the Chiricahua Apache chief, Cochise. Just to the west of the Dragoons lies the infamous town of Tombstone, where Wyatt Earp and Doc Holliday shot it out with the Cowboy Gang in 1881.

On the northern flanks of the Huachucas is Fort Huachuca, originally established as an outpost in 1877 to protect settlers from Apache Indians. Fort Huachuca is the nation's only remaining cavalry fort that is still an active army post today. The Buffalo Soldiers, famed black cavalry and infantry troops, were often stationed at Ft. Huachuca, and played an active role in the history of Arizona Territory.

Farther to the north, lying parallel to Highway 90, are the Whetstone Mountains and Kartchner Caverns State Park. To the northwest you can see the Arizona Trail corridor. The Santa Rita Mountains are visible north of Sonoita, then the Rincons, and far in the distance, the Santa Catalina Mountains rise up from the Sonoran Desert northeast of Tucson. The string of mountain peaks disappears into the blue horizon, leading Arizona Trail travelers on toward the distant Grand Canyon and the Utah border.

To the west is the faraway glimmer of Parker Canyon Lake, nestled into the rolling Canelo Hills. Looking southwest, see the vast Spanish land grants - the grasslands of the San Raphael Valley and Mexico.

Having gone full-circle, it's time to relax and enjoy the great views. Apache Indians, Spanish explorers, Buffalo Soldiers and bandits may have all, at one time or another, sat on the same rock and admired the view that is yours today.

Sweeping views and interpretive signs greet visitors to Montezuma Pass.

CORONADO
NATIONAL MEMORIAL

Located in the Huachuca Mountains on the United States/Mexico border, Coronado National Memorial was established in 1952, to commemorate the first major exploration of Europeans into what is now the American Southwest.

During the early decades of the 16th century, Spain established a prosperous colonial empire in the New World, from Mexico to Peru. Tales were told of riches in unknown lands to the north. Cities with streets lined with goldsmith shops, houses of many stories, and doorways studded with turquoise and emeralds had been reported to Viceroy Mendoza of New Spain by earlier explorers.

In 1540 Francisco Vasquez de Coronado was commissioned by the Viceroy to lead an expedition in search of the "Seven Cities of Cibola". Coronado began his journey in February of 1540 with over 300 Spanish soldiers, several hundred Indian allies and fifteen hundred stock animals.

Although they did not discover the "cities of gold", members of Coronado's party did discover the Grand Canyon and numerous Indian cultures. Coronado made it all the way to what is now Kansas before abandoning his quest and returning to Mexico in disgrace. He died at forty-two, never knowing the ramifications of his amazing journey, which paved the way for later Spanish explorers and missionaries to colonize the Southwest.

Coronado National Memorial has the distinction of being either the very beginning or the very end of the statewide Arizona Trail (depending on which direction you are travelling). The Yaqui Ridge Trail (Trip 18) is the Arizona Trail's southernmost segment.

The visitor center, open from 8:00 am to 5:00 pm every day except Thanksgiving and Christmas, has a small museum and bookstore. The picnic area, open only during daylight hours, has tables, grills, water and restrooms. Overnight camping is not permitted. Bicycles are permitted on roads, but not on any trails within the Memorial.

Coronado National Memorial is adjacent to the international border where illegal immigration and drug smuggling activities may be present. Report any suspicious activities to a Park Ranger, visit during daylight hours only and always bring a hiking partner with you. Camping is not allowed within the memorial, and is not recommended in the National Forest that borders the memorial.

Stone steps lead to the entrance of Coronado Cave

TRIP 16

CORONADO CAVE TRAIL

This trip offers visitors an energetic hike up the side of Montezuma Peak, to explore a cave that is completely undeveloped. While Coronado Cave can't compare to Kartchner Caverns, either in size, or in the variety of its mineral formations, it offers a different kind of adventure.

Coronado Cave is unimproved – as wild now as when it was used as a hideout by Apache Indians. There are no lights or maintained trails within the cave. Entering the cave involves climbing up over large boulders, and then climbing carefully down through sometimes-slippery rocks to the floor of the cavern.

Permits to visit the cave are required, but they are free at the visitor center, which is open from 8:00 am to 5:00 pm. While registering for a permit, hikers will be given a handout of rules, which are enforced to protect the fragile environment of the cave. Flashlights are required and the center suggests that you bring one per person, and allow a minimum of two hours for the visit.

Bicycles, horses *and* ***pets*** *are not allowed on any of the Coronado Memorial trails described in this book.*

DRIVING DISTANCE FROM KCSP: 41 miles

LOCATION: Coronado National Memorial

LENGTH: 1.5 miles roundtrip

RATING: Difficult with an elevation gain of 470 feet in 0.7 miles.

CONTACT AGENCY: Coronado National Memorial (520) 366-5515

GETTING THERE: Passenger car. From KCSP drive south on Highway 90 for 18.7 miles, passing through Huachuca City, to the 90 bypass which is marked by a stoplight. Turn left, and travel 4.5 miles to Fry Boulevard. (Highway 90/92 junction). Here, Highway 90 turns left (east). Continue straight across the intersection (south) on Highway 92 for

MAP 9
CORONADO NATIONAL MEMORIAL
16 - Coronado Cave Trail
17 - Joe's Canyon Trail
18 - Yaqui Ridge (Arizona Trail)
19 - Coronado Peak Trail

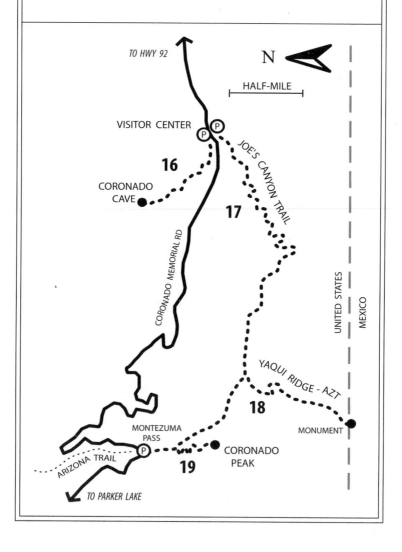

13 miles, to Coronado Memorial Road. Turn right (south) toward the memorial. Follow the paved road 5 miles to the visitor center. The trail leaves from the west end of the parking lot.

TRAIL DESCRIPTION:

The rock-lined trail leaves the parking area, wandering through a woodland of oaks, junipers and sycamore trees, as it follows along the left bank of a drainage. Looming overhead on the right is Montezuma Peak. The trail begins to climb, winding up through a series of steps made of wooden timbers set into the side of the hill. As the trail climbs, there are nice views of the road below and wild, rugged Montezuma Canyon.

The trail levels briefly in a grassy area dotted with manzanita trees, oaks and seasonal wild flowers. This is a chance to catch your breath before the next steep climb.

The route follows a dry creek bed, which could become flooded in a heavy rain. The trail, which is shaded much of the way, winds among white limestone boulders. The drainage is lined with oaks, bear grass and yuccas. A series of rock steps leads the final distance to the cave entrance.

As you look down into darkness on a warm day, you can feel the cooler air of the cavern. Watch your footing, and look out for low overhangs. It's time to break out the flashlights and explore.

JOE'S CANYON TRAIL

Joe's Canyon Trail is a steep but scenic climb from the visitor center to the parking area on top of Montezuma Pass. Joe's Canyon Trail provides access to two other trails described in this chapter – the Yaqui Ridge Trail (Trip 18) and the Coronado Peak Trail (Trip 19).

***Bicycles**, **horses** and **pets** are not allowed on any of the Coronado Memorial trails described in this book.*

DRIVING DISTANCE FROM KCSP: 41 miles

LOCATION: Coronado National Memorial.

LENGTH: 3.1 miles one way. A second vehicle can be left either at the picnic area across from the visitor center, or at Montezuma Pass for a one-way hike.

RATING: Difficult with an elevation gain of 1,320 feet.

CONTACT AGENCY: Coronado National Memorial (520) 366-5515

GETTING THERE: Passenger car. From KCSP drive south on Highway 90 for 18.7 miles, passing through Huachuca City, to the 90 bypass which is marked by a stoplight. Turn left, and travel 4.5 miles to Fry Boulevard (Highway 90/92 junction). Here, Highway 90 turns left (east). Continue straight across the intersection (south) on Highway 92 for 13 miles, to Coronado Memorial Road. Turn right (south) toward the Memorial. Follow the paved road for 5 miles to the visitor center. Joe's Canyon trailhead is across the road from the visitor center.

TRAIL DESCRIPTION:

Joe's Canyon Trail begins at the road junction with the picnic area across from the visitor center. The well-maintained trail switchbacks up through a beautiful canyon, gaining 1,000 feet in the first mile. The trail offers scenic views of Joe's Canyon, Montezuma Canyon, and the San Pedro Valley. After reaching a saddle at the top of windswept Smuggler's Ridge, the trail continues westward with southerly views into the grasslands of Sonora, Mexico.

2.3 miles from the parking area, the trail passes a junction with the Yaqui Ridge Trail. This is the first segment of the statewide Arizona Trail that travels from Mexico to Utah. The Yaqui Ridge Trail drops south for 1 mile to the U.S./ Mexico border, which is marked by a barbed wire fence and a seven-foot high iron and concrete monument.

Joe's Canyon Trail, now part of the route of the Arizona Trail, continues around the northeastern side of Coronado Peak where it joins the Coronado Peak Trail, 200 hundred yards from the Montezuma Pass parking lot.

TRIP 18

YAQUI RIDGE TRAIL

The Yaqui Ridge Trail has the distinction of being, (depending on which direction you are traveling), either the very beginning or the very end of the statewide Arizona Trail. It is the Arizona Trail's southernmost segment, beginning in a windswept saddle by the barbed wire fence and historic seven foot-high monument that marks the United States/Mexico border.

There are no roads into this remote area along the border. The Yaqui Ridge Trail climbs steeply from the border fence to Smuggler's Ridge where it joins Joe's Canyon Trail, which becomes the route of the Arizona Trail as it continues on to the Montezuma Pass parking area. From the parking area the Arizona Trail continues north through the Huachuca Mountains. (See Trips 15, 21, 22, 23, 24, and 30 for other connections to the Arizona Trail).

***Bicycles, horses** and **pets** are not allowed on the Yaqui Ridge or Joe's Canyon Trails.*

DRIVING DISTANCE FROM KCSP: 44 miles

LOCATION: Coronado National Memorial. From the Montezuma Pass parking area to the United States/Mexico border fence.

LENGTH: 3.5 miles round trip.

RATING: Difficult, with an elevation loss and gain of 750 feet.

CONTACT AGENCY: Coronado National Memorial (520) 366-5515

GETTING THERE: Passenger car. From KCSP drive south on Highway 90 for 18.7 miles, passing through Huachuca City, to the 90 bypass, which is marked by a stoplight. Turn left, and travel 4.5 miles to Fry Boulevard, (Highway 90/92 junction). Here, Highway 90 turns left (east). Continue straight across the intersection (south) on Highway 92 for 13 miles, to Coronado Memorial Road. Turn right (south)

A monument marks the United States/Mexico border. Arizona Trail Yaqui Ridge dedication, 1998. Dale Shewalter, AZT founder and Pam Gluck, American Trails.

toward the memorial. Follow the paved road past the visitor center. Soon, the pavement is replaced with a narrow dirt road, which is steep with hairpin turns. This road can be icy and occasionally closes in the winter. The road tops out at Montezuma Pass, a scenic overlook with a paved parking area and rest rooms.

TRAIL DESCRIPTION:

Starting from the ramada at Montezuma Pass, follow the Coronado Peak/Joe's Canyon Trail south. This is also the route of the Arizona Trail. At 0.1 miles is a junction where the Coronado Peak Trail branches off to the right. Stay on the Joe's Canyon/Arizona Trail as it traverses the east side of Coronado Peak and follows Smuggler's Ridge to a junction with the Yaqui Ridge Trail.

The Yaqui Ridge Trail branches to the right and descends a hillside that affords sweeping views of Sonora Mexico and the San Pedro Valley. The route drops steeply, and switchbacks toward a grassy, windswept saddle. The hike ends at the international border - a barbed wire fence, with the monument just beyond. The fence to the right marks the National Monument/Coronado National Forest boundary. Stick your toe under the border fence and you can say that you have been in Mexico today. Return the way that you came.

TRIP 19

CORONADO PEAK TRAIL

Coronado National Memorial was established to commemorate Francisco Vasquez de Coronado's journey of 1540, the first major exploration of Europeans into what is now the United States. The visitor center has a small museum with authentic 16th century Spanish armor and weaponry, paintings, and a video which tells the story of the expedition.

Coronado Peak Trail affords not only spectacular views of the route that Coronado is thought to have taken, but an intriguing glimpse into the lives of the conquistadors as they traveled north. The National Memorial has done a great job of providing signage, with actual quotations from the expedition journals, along the trail.

Bicycles, horses *and* **pets** *are not allowed on any of the Coronado Memorial trails described in this book.*

DRIVING DISTANCE FROM KCSP: 44 miles

LOCATION: Coronado National Memorial. The trail travels from the Montezuma Pass parking area to the top of Coronado Peak.

LENGTH: 0.8 miles round trip

RATING: Moderate. The trail has steep switchbacks, however there are frequent benches for resting.

A winter hike to Coronado Peak

CONTACT AGENCY: Coronado National Memorial
(520) 366-5515

GETTING THERE: Passenger car. From KCSP drive south on Highway 90 for 18.7 miles, passing through Huachuca City, to the 90 bypass, which is marked by a stoplight. Turn left, and travel 4.5 miles to Fry Boulevard, (Highway 90/92 junction). Here, Highway 90 turns left (east). Continue straight across the intersection (south) on Highway 92 for 13 miles, to Coronado Memorial Road. Turn right (south) toward the memorial. Follow the paved road past the visitor center. Soon, the pavement is replaced with a narrow dirt road, which is steep with hairpin turns. This road can be icy and occasionally closes in the winter. The road tops out at Montezuma Pass, a scenic overlook with a paved parking area and rest rooms.

TRAIL DESCRIPTION:

The trail that travels south from the ramada at Montezuma Pass, is actually three in one! This is the route for not only the Coronado Peak Trail, but also Joe's Canyon Trail and the Arizona Trail, which travels to the United States/Mexico border as the Yaqui Ridge segment. At 0.1 miles is a junction. Follow the Coronado Peak Trail to the right.

The Coronado Peak Trail offers spacious views of Sonora Mexico and the valley of the San Pedro River, thought to be the route of Coronado's expedition of 1540. As the trail becomes steeper, thoughtfully-placed benches and interpretive signs, both in English and Spanish, are a welcome excuse to stop and catch your breath.

The historic view has changed little in the past 450 years. It's easy to imagine the scene: over 300 Spanish soldiers on horseback with their metal armor and helmets glinting in the sun, accompanied by several hundred Indian troops and over a thousand stock animals, making their way along the San Pedro Valley.

At the top of the peak, a ramada affords hikers a welcome rest in the shade while enjoying the panoramic views. Return the way that you came.

An equestrian's dream: miles of grassy rangeland to explore.

LAS CIENEGAS NATIONAL CONSERVATION AREA and the Empire Ranch

Cattle have grazed the rolling grasslands of what is now the Las Cienegas National Conservation Area for over 300 years, beginning in 1699 when Father Kino, a Jesuit missionary and explorer, delivered 150 head of cattle to the headwaters of Sonoita Creek, near Patagonia.

In 1876, Walter Vail purchased the land as a 160-acre ranch. He soon acquired adjacent land, some of which later became the Cienega Ranch, named for Cienega Creek, a year-round water source. By 1905 the ranch had spread to 1,000 square miles over two counties and had, indeed, become an empire.

Between 1880 and 1885 Vail and other partners successfully operated the Total Wreck silver mine in the northern part of the ranch. In its heyday the operation supported a community of 300 people. All that remains of Total Wreck today are mine tailings and old foundations.

The property was owned by a real estate developer and a mining company before a series of land exchanges in 1988 brought the land into public ownership under the administration of the Bureau of Land Management.

The picturesque old adobe ranch house and buildings are undergoing restoration by the Empire Ranch Foundation in partnership with the BLM. Long-range plans may include a visitor center with exhibits and educational programs, a picnic area and an interpretive trail.

This high desert setting supports an excellent example of native grasslands. Pronghorn antelope are often seen in the rolling landscape of the conservation area. Once native to the area, the pronghorns were reintroduced in 1981. About 230 species of birds have been identified in the area. The grasslands are also home to mule and white tail deer, javelinas, badgers, coatimundis, ringtail cats, gila monsters and many other animals.

TRIP 20

SOUTH ROAD
to the EMPIRE RANCH

South Road, EC-900, is an unpaved road that travels through the rolling grasslands of the Las Cienegas National Conservation Area to the historic Empire Ranch. While this is a road, rather than a trail, we have included it because it is scenic, and especially popular with **bicyclists** *and* **equestrians**.

The adobe ranch house and buildings are undergoing restoration by the Empire Ranch Foundation in partnership with the BLM. Since this area is still a working ranch, please do not disturb cattle or horses.

DRIVING DISTANCE FROM KCSP: 25 miles

LOCATION: Las Cienegas National Conservation Area

Watch for pronghorn antelope in the grasslands

LENGTH: 8.5 miles one way. If driving, high clearance vehicles are recommended.

RATING: Easy

CONTACT AGENCY: Bureau of Land Management (520) 722-4289.

GETTING THERE: High-clearance vehicles recommended. Travel south from KCSP for 10 miles to Highway 82. Turn right (west) and drive 15 miles, past mile marker 37, to the LCNCA gate, which is set back on the right (north) side of the road.

You can return the same way, or have someone meet you at the ranch. Bicyclists may want to make a loop by continuing west from the ranch for 3 miles to Highway 83. Travel south on 83 for 6.5 miles to Sonoita, and then east on Highway 82 for 4.2 miles to the starting point, for a total of 22.2 miles.

ROUTE DESCRIPTION:

As you follow South Road (EC 900) north, watch for pronghorn antelope. Once native to the area, the pronghorns were reintroduced in 1981. The route affords nice views of the western side of the Whetstone Mountains. Kartchner Caverns State Park is located on the east side of this range. On the left, or west horizon, are the Santa Rita Mountains and 9,453-foot Mount Wrightson.

A little over 4 miles from Highway 82 is a junction with a road that travels toward some distant cottonwood trees. Stay to the left. 6 miles from the starting point the road travels through Gardner Canyon Wash, an area of large mesquite and cottonwood trees. The road winds through an area of wooden corrals and pens before climbing up a steep hill out of the wash.

8.3 miles from its beginning, South Road arrives at a junction with Empire-Cienega Road, EC-901. Turn left and travel 0.2 miles to the Empire Ranch headquarters.

You may want to have someone pick you up at the ranch, rather than backtracking. The ranch can be reached from Highway 83, by traveling north from Sonoita for 6.5 miles to the National Conservation Area road. Drive for 3 miles to the ranch.

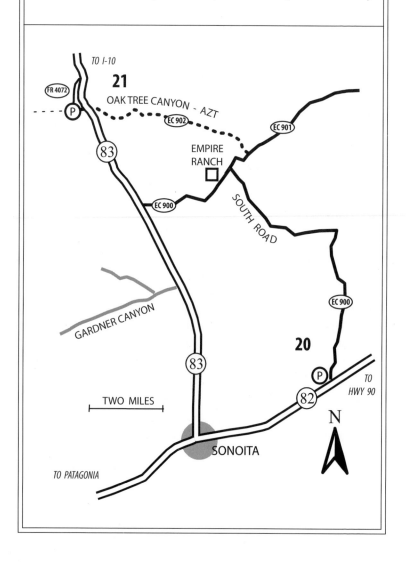

MAP 10
LAS CIENEGAS NATIONAL
CONSERVATION AREA
20 - South Road to Empire Ranch
21 - Oak Tree Canyon to Empire Ranch (Arizona Trail)

*The rolling hills of the old Empire Ranch, with the
Whetstone Mountains on the horizon*

TRIP 21

OAK TREE CANYON
to the EMPIRE RANCH

*Oak Tree Canyon once boasted the largest Emory oak tree
in Arizona. Unfortunately, the tree was toppled during winds
generated by Hurricane Lester in 1998. The trip follows a fairly
level dirt road, great for* **biking** *or* **horses**. *This pleasant route
travels through rolling grasslands dotted with oak trees, to
the historic Empire Ranch.*

*The buildings are undergoing restoration by the Empire
Ranch foundation in partnership with the BLM. You may visit
the buildings but remember that this is not only a historic site,
but also a working ranch. Do not remove artifacts or disturb
livestock. A site host is sometimes present. This is a nice one-
way trip if you leave a vehicle at the ranch, or arrange for
someone to meet you.*

At time of printing, this trip follows the proposed route of the border-to-border Arizona Trail, through Las Cienegas National Conservation Area. However, the AZT route beyond this trip has not been completed. The AZT also travels south from the Oak Tree Canyon trailhead to Kentucky Camp, and on to Mexico. (See Trips 22 and 23).

DRIVING DISTANCE FROM KCSP: 39.5 miles.

LOCATION: Oak Tree Canyon and Highway 83, north of Sonoita.

LENGTH: 6.4 miles one way

RATING: Easy

CONTACT AGENCY: Bureau of Land Management (520) 722-4289.

GETTING THERE: Oak Tree Canyon Trailhead: Travel south from KCSP for 10 miles to Highway 82. Turn right (west) and drive 19.5 miles to Sonoita. Turn right (north) on Highway 83 and drive for 10 miles (you will have passed the road into

Original structures survive at the ranch headquarters

the Empire Ranch at 6.5 miles). Turn into the parking area on the left (FR 4072), just past milepost 43. It is easy to miss because there is no sign on the highway. In the spacious parking area a large sign tells about the Arizona Trail, which also travels south from here to Kentucky Camp.

Empire Ranch: The turnoff to the National Conservation Area is on Hwy 83, 6.5 miles north of Sonoita, on the right or east side of the highway. It is 3 miles on a gravel road to the ranch.

TRAIL DESCRIPTION:

The trail leaves the parking area, traveling under Highway 83 through a cement culvert that is large enough for equestrians. As the trail passes through a Forest Service gate, it joins a dirt road heading east. This is ranchland, so be sure to close this and all gates that you pass through.

At junctions, stay on the main, more-traveled road, heading east toward the Whetstone Mountains. For better views of the surrounding countryside you can hike up and follow along the ridgeline to the south of the road.

1.7 miles from the parking area is a cattle guard and a gate. This is the boundary between the National Forest and the Bureau of Land Management. The road, now EC-902, continues through an area of mesquite trees, passing a windmill tower and a large cement water tank. Farther on, a shady grove of huge oak trees offers a welcome place to take a break.

4.5 miles from the trailhead the road crosses a gas line road. A half-mile farther the road curves to the southeast, passes a large ramada on the left, and ends at a junction with Empire-Cienega Road, EC-901. Looking to the west, you can see the ranch headquarters, three quarters of-a-mile away. Turn right (west) and follow the Empire-Cienega Road to the ranch. Watch for motorized traffic on this pretty stretch of road as it winds under some enormous Cottonwood trees, and crosses Empire Gulch.

Return the way that you came, or have someone meet you at the ranch. See *Getting There* directions to the Empire Ranch.

There's lots to see in the Santa Rita Mountain foothills
Courtesy Kate Ladson

SANTA RITA MOUNTAINS

The Santa Rita Mountains, dominated by 9,453-foot Mount Wrightson, are another excellent example of an Arizona Sky Island. Some believe that it was Father Kino, a Spanish priest, who named the Santa Ritas when he visited the area in the late 1600s.

Gold was discovered on the east slope of the Santa Ritas in 1874, in what proved to be the largest and richest placer deposit in southern Arizona. Hundreds of miners flocked to the area. Placer deposits consist of small bits of gold mixed with sand and gravel, and the best way to separate the gold from the sand is with water. But water was a scarce and valuable commodity.

In 1902 California mining engineer James Stetson came up with a plan to channel runoff from the mountain's snowmelt into a reservoir that would hold enough water for a placer mine operation. Stetson found investors and formed the Santa Rita Water and Mining Company. In 1903 they built an 8.5 mile-long water system. The adobe buildings of Kentucky Camp, built in 1904, served as the mine company's headquarters. After expending $200,000 on the project, they had only extracted a few thousand dollars worth of gold when Stetson was killed in a fall from a Tucson hotel window. Financial support faltered, and the operation folded.

Gardner Canyon is named for Thomas Gardner, who established a ranch at Apache Spring in 1872. Despite frequent raids by Apache Indians, Gardner and his family lived there for more than twenty years.

The state-wide Arizona Trail has a trailhead just beyond Apache Springs Ranch on Gardner Canyon Road. The Arizona Trail, coming north from Patagonia, follows the route of Stetson's water system from Big Casa Blanca Canyon to Kentucky Camp.

Madera Canyon, on the northwest side of the Santa Ritas, is renowned for its bird life, including some rare, sub-tropical species like the elegant trogon. There are nature walks, rental cabins, a gift shop, and excellent hiking opportunities.

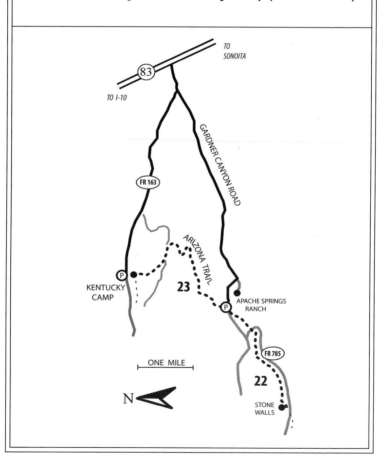

MAP 11
SANTA RITA MOUNTAIN FOOTHILLS
22 - The Ditch Trail (Arizona Trail)
23 - Gardner Canyon to Kentucky Camp (Arizona Trail)

TRIP 22

THE DITCH TRAIL

At the turn of the 18th century, an aqueduct was constructed to carry water for over eight and a half miles from Bear Spring, in Big Casa Blanca Canyon, to a hydraulic mining operation near Kentucky Gulch. Heading south from Gardner Canyon, this pleasant trail, (also known as the China Man Trail) wanders an almost-level course as it follows the old aqueduct across the canyon-cut landscape. The Forest Service has done a great job of restoring and placing interpretive signs on this historic trail that is now a part of the state-wide Arizona Trail.

*This is a great trail for **bicycles** and **horses**. Leashed **dogs** are allowed.*

DRIVING DISTANCE FROM KCSP: 38 miles

LOCATION: Santa Rita Mountain foothills

LENGTH: 4.4 miles roundtrip

RATING: Easy

CONTACT AGENCY: Coronado National Forest, Nogales Ranger District (520) 281-2296

GETTING THERE: Passenger car. Travel south from KCSP for 10 miles to Highway 82. Turn right (west) and drive 19.5 miles to Sonoita. Turn right (north) on Highway 83 and drive 4 miles to Gardner Canyon Road on the left. Follow Gardner Canyon Road 4.5 miles to an unsigned junction with the road into Apache Springs Ranch. Stay to the right and travel another 0.3 miles to the Arizona Trail parking area.

TRAIL DESCRIPTION:

The trail exits the Arizona Trail parking area in Gardner Canyon, on the west. Heading directly toward the Santa Rita Mountains, the route affords a nice view of Mount Wrightson, the mountain's highest peak with an elevation of 9,453 feet. The trail adjoins Gardner Canyon Road for a short distance, then leaves the road on the left (south).

The rock-lined path drops down through oak trees to a

gate, and a small creek. The trail crosses the creek and climbs the bank to a second gate. The route is south through a level, grassy area, dotted with small juniper trees to another gate and corrals. Just past here is a junction. Watch for the Arizona Trail (AZT) sign where the trail forks to the right (west).

At 0.7 miles the trail crosses Forest Road 785, then travels uphill through a woodland of oak and juniper. The trail levels, and soon after arrives at an interpretive sign marking where the trail adjoins "the ditch". Water traveled in the ditch to this point, and was then transported via a metal pipeline to Boston Gulch, near what is now the ghost town of Kentucky Camp.

The trail follows the ditch along a high ridgeline, a pleasant section that is almost level with a slight downhill grade. Heading directly toward the Santa Ritas, it is high enough to provide spacious views.

A mile and a half from the trailhead the route drops down to wind through a pretty little arroyo. At the slightly lower elevation, juniper is replaced by manzanita and yucca, and oak trees offer welcome shade.

A half-mile farther the trail passes between a natural rock face and old stone walls – once part of a dam that stood ten feet high and one hundred feet long. This dam held thousands of gallons of water needed for the hydraulic mining operation in Boston Gulch, near Kentucky Camp. This is a pretty place, with small, clear pools of water and the picturesque old stone walls.

It is a short distance to another interpretive sign that tells the story of the ditch, then another 0.1 miles to a second junction with FR 785. Turn around here and return the way that you came, or follow the Arizona Trail south. It is 19.5 miles to Patagonia, and 55 miles to Mexico. (Bicycles are not allowed in the Mount Wrightson Wilderness).

TRIP 23

GARDNER CANYON
to KENTUCKY CAMP

This segment of the statewide Arizona Trail follows high ridgelines through the rolling foothills of the Santa Rita Mountains, from Gardner Canyon north to the ghost town of Kentucky Camp. Part of the trip parallels the route of the long-abandoned Santa Rita Water and Mining Company pipeline that once supplied water for the hydraulic mining venture that was Kentucky Camp.

*The trail, which is popular with mountain **bicyclists** and **equestrians**, affords sweeping vistas of rolling grasslands and surrounding mountain ranges before dropping into Fish Canyon and swinging back to the ghost town. Leashed **dogs** are allowed.*

The original adobe buildings have been beautifully restored by the Forest Service and by a volunteer organization, the "Friends of Kentucky Camp". Site hosts live at the camp, and if you would like to spend a night in a ghost town, one of the adobes has been renovated as a "Bed no Breakfast."

A one-way hike or ride may be made from Gardner Canyon Road, by leaving a vehicle at the parking area above Kentucky Camp.

For those who would like a short but steep one-half mile (roundtrip) walk into Kentucky Camp, see GETTING THERE for directions. The drive into Kentucky Camp is beautiful, and also a favorite with bicyclists.

DRIVING DISTANCE FROM KCSP: 38 miles

LOCATION: Gardner Canyon in Santa Rita foothills

LENGTH: 3.6 miles one way.

RATING: Easy to moderate

CONTACT AGENCY: Coronado National Forest, Nogales Ranger District (520) 281-2296.

GETTING THERE: Travel south from KCSP for 10 miles to

Highway 82. Turn right (west) and drive 19.5 miles to Sonoita. Turn right (north) on Highway 83 and drive 4 miles to Gardner Canyon Road on the left. Passing a junction with FR 163 (which is signed for Kentucky Camp), follow Gardner Canyon Road 4.5 miles to a junction with the drive going into Apache Springs Ranch. Stay to the right and travel another 0.3 miles to the Arizona Trail parking area.

Driving to Kentucky Camp: After turning off of Highway 83 onto Gardner Canyon Road, drive 0.8 miles to the first junction, FR 163, which is signed Fish Canyon and Kentucky Camp. Turn right and follow the signs for five miles to the parking area above Kentucky Camp. It is a steep quarter mile walk from the parking area down to the ghost town.

Some may opt, after following FR 163 for 2.2 miles, to unload bikes or horses at the National Forest boundary, for an enjoyable (mostly uphill) ride through rolling grassland to Kentucky Camp.

TRAIL DESCRIPTION:

The trail leaves the north end of the Gardner Canyon parking area and climbs steeply to the top of a ridge, affording a nice view back to the south. This is the most difficult part of the hike – the rest is almost all down hill.

The route is to the left, adjoining an old dirt road for a few yards, then forking off to the right, passing over a partially exposed section of old metal pipe. The trail passes a Forest Service interpretive sign that explains how the stone foundations along the trail were used to elevate and support the pipes crossing over small drainages.

0.8 miles from the trailhead the path climbs to a higher ridgeline, and a junction with a dirt road. The route leaves the pipeline here, turning right (east) to travel along the long, grassy slope, toward the distant Whetstone Mountains. After going half a mile, look to the left (north) for a glimpse of the adobe buildings of Kentucky Camp, nestled into the grassy folds of the gulch.

After following the ridgeline for one mile, watch for the AZT marker where the trail leaves the old road on the left (north), dropping down through oak-canopied switchbacks into the broad, grassy drainage of Fish Canyon. This is a pretty area, rimmed with rolling hills. Passing through a gate, the trail then crosses FR 4085. Turning west onto a closed dirt road, the route continues to another gate. After passing through the gate the trail follows the fence a short distance, past some interpretive signs to Kentucky Camp.

From Kentucky Camp the Arizona Trail continues north for 10.8 miles to the Oak Tree Canyon trailhead.

Volunteers have restored much of Kentucky Camp

KENTUCKY CAMP
to OAK TREE CANYON

Beginning at the historic ghost town of Kentucky Camp, this portion of the statewide Arizona Trail follows a series of old roads and trails through the rolling foothills of the Santa Rita Mountains.

*This segment of the Arizona Trail is popular with mountain **bicyclists** and **equestrians.** Leashed **dogs** are allowed. A one way trip can be made, by leaving a vehicle at the Oak Tree Canyon trailhead, where there are spacious parking areas for turning horsetrailers.*

MAP 12
SANTA RITA MOUNTAIN FOOTHILLS
24 - Kentucky Camp to Oak Tree Canyon (Arizona Trail)

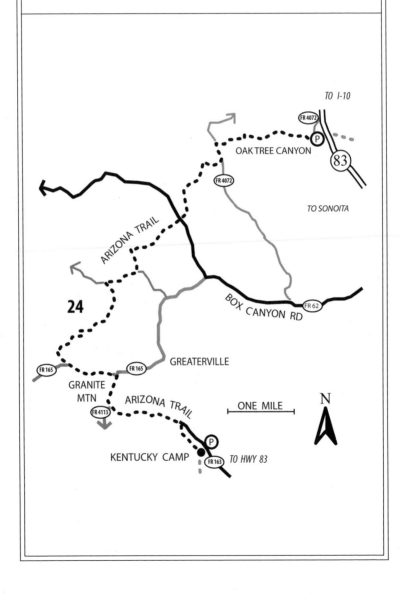

The Oak Tree Trailhead was initially developed for the Arizona Trail, a non-motorized pathway across the state. Unfortunatly, the trailhead has become very popular with all-terrain vehicle enthusiasts, creating some user conflicts in the area. Since the sounds of ATVs may intrude upon the solitude and the quality of the outdoor experience that non-motorized trail users are seeking, the author recommends avoiding Oak Tree Canyon on weekends.

DRIVING DISTANCE FROM KCSP: 39 miles

LOCATION: The Santa Rita foothills

LENGTH: 10.8 miles one way.

RATING: Easy to moderate

CONTACT AGENCY: Coronado National Forest, Nogales Ranger District (520) 281-2296.

GETTING THERE: Travel south from KCSP for 10 miles to Highway 82. Turn right (west) and drive 19.5 miles to Sonoita. Turn right (north) on Highway 83 and drive 4 miles to Gardner Canyon Road on the left. Follow Gardner Canyon 0.8 miles to a junction with FR 163, which is signed for Kentucky Camp. Follow FR 163 for 5 miles to the parking area and gate above Kentucky Camp. It is a steep quarter mile walk from the parking area down to the ghost town.

To reach the Oak Tree Canyon trailhead, instead of turning onto Gardner Canyon Road, continue north on Highway 83. 10 miles north of Sonoita turn left on FR 4072 into the parking area. The turnoff is just past milepost 43 and is easy to miss because there is no sign on the highway.

TRAIL DESCRIPTION:

From the parking area above Kentucky Camp, pass through the gate and follow the road downhill a quarter-mile to the ghost town. Take the time to visit and enjoy the buildings that have been restored by the Forest Service and a volunteer organization, "Friends of Kentucky Camp". A site host is usually present.

Pick up the Arizona Trail as it exits Kentucky Camp through a gate on the west end of the camp. The trail follows Kentucky Gulch for a half mile before veering uphill to the right, to connect with FR 163.

Continue on FR 163 as it travels west, along a high ridgeline, toward the Santa Rita Mountains. There is a nice view of Mt. Wrightson on the left and the distant Rincon Mountains on the right. The Whetstone Mountains, home of Kartchner Caverns, are behind or east, and the Santa Rita foothills roll away in all directions.

Passing through a gate and a junction with FR 4113, continue on FR 163 as it heads uphill, curving north, around the base of Granite Mountain. There are occasional stock tanks along this section.

2.2 miles from Kentucky Camp the road makes a sharp left. Disregard the "Dead End" sign and follow the road down a wash, heading north to a junction with FR 165 (the Old Greaterville Road). FR 163 ends here.

Turn left (west) on FR 165 and travel 0.9 miles to a large AZT sign marking the turnoff onto an old road on the right. As the road climbs the hill, look down to the left. There is a small pond nestled in the fold of the hills below. Turn right at the rock cairn and continue up the hill to a high ridgeline, heading east toward the Whetstones. Take a moment to catch your breath and enjoy the fabulous views.

4 miles from Kentucky Camp the route passes through a gate, then drops down a grassy ridgeline, heading northeast. The trail follows a fence as it winds down through an oak woodland to the grassy floor of Enzenberg Canyon. Cross the drainage to an AZT sign and turn left (west) onto a little-used dirt road. Notice the power lines overhead. In 0.3 miles, the road intersects a well-used 4WD road. Turn right (east), following the route as it winds down through oak and juniper trees to the grassy floor of a drainage.

Lucky visitors may spot wildlife along the trail. Here a coyote trots through the grass in search of a meal.

At 6.7 miles, the two-track enters a big open meadow. As the track continues across the meadow, stay to the right, following a path east toward a large gateway. Don't pass through the fence, but follow AZT signs guiding you north. The path takes you through a beautiful, grassy, oak-lined drainage and then up a wooded hillside to a junction with the Madera Canyon/Box Canyon Road, FR 62.

After crossing the road, the trail ascends a grass ridgeline and travels for 0.9 miles to a dirt road. Once the route of the AZT, this is now also an ATV road. From here to Oak Tree Canyon be on the alert for ATV traffic. Turn left (or north), heading uphill. There are nice views of the Helvetia Hills to the north and the Whetstones to the east. It is only 0.3 miles to the junction with FR 4072.

Turn left (northwest) on FR 4072 through a fence gateway made of rail road ties. Follow the road for 0.2 miles to a junction. At this point the road drops steeply to the left. A sign indicates where our route, the AZT, branches off to the right (east) ascending a steep hillside. From the summit of the hill there are great views of the Mustang Mountains, the Huachuca Mountains and Mexico, to the south.

After 0.4 miles, turn left on a dirt road which travels down to a large white tank and a power line. Just before the tank turn right and travel downhill into Oak Tree Canyon. Once down on the level, watch for an unsigned road junction. Stay left, traveling past a stock pond to the trailhead.

For many people, the Saguaro symbolizes the desert

SAGUARO NATIONAL PARK

Saguaro National Park has a unique "forest" different from any other in North America. The park was established in 1933 to protect an extraordinary and picturesque plant - the giant saguaro cactus of the Sonoran Desert. The saguaro's white blossoms, which appear April through June, are Arizona's state flower.

Saguaros are slow growing, taking fifty years to reach a height of seven feet. The plant may take seventy-five years to sprout its first "arm". Saguaros can reach heights of fifty feet and weigh up to eight tons. Despite their massive size, saguaro cactus are very fragile. Freezing weather, extended droughts, vandalism, and cactus thieves take their toll. The longnose bat, which plays an important part in pollinating the cactus, is rapidly losing its winter habitat in Mexico, another threat to the continued existence of saguaros.

The Park offers two visitor centers (East and West), guided tours, a barrier-free nature walk, scenic drives, picnic areas and hiking, biking and equestrian trails. This is classic Sonoran Desert at its best. There is a nominal fee when entering Saguaro National Park East from the visitor center. The scenic loop drive closes at sunset.

Summer midday temperatures may reach as high as 120 degrees Fahrenheit. Walk during the cooler part of the day, wear a hat and sunscreen, and take plenty of water.

Bicycles are allowed only on the paved Cactus Forest Loop Drive, and the 2.5-mile section of the Cactus Forest Trail that is within the Loop Drive.

Equestrians should use the trailhead located at the end of Broadway, as horse trailers are not allowed at the visitor center or on the Loop Drive.

MAP 13
SAGUARO NATIONAL PARK - EAST
25 - Cactus Forest Loop Drive
26 - Cactus Forest Trail
27 - Desert Ecology Trail

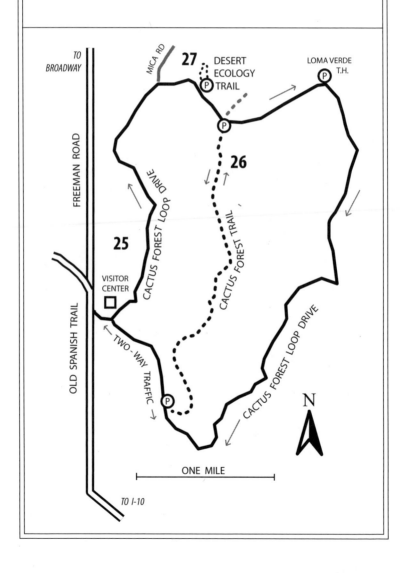

TRIP 25

CACTUS FOREST LOOP DRIVE

Saguaro National Park East offers bicyclists the opportunity to view the spectacular scenery of the Sonoran Desert in two specially designated areas. Beginning at the visitor center, which has provided a shade ramada, water fountain and bicycle rack, we recommend that you pick up a copy of the park's free bicycling brochure.

The Cactus Forest Loop Drive, which closes at sunset, is a scenic route through the lower elevations of the park. The loop drive, a one-way road for the first 6.5 miles, is open to motorized vehicles and joggers as well as bicyclists. The drive is narrow with many tight turns and steep hills. Slow down before curves or hills, and in congested areas such as the visitor center and picnic areas.

Bicycles *are also allowed on a 2.5-mile section of the Cactus Forest Trail that is located within the loop drive. (See Trip 26).* ***Pets*** *are not allowed on trails within the park.*

DRIVING DISTANCE FROM KCSP: 45 miles to the park entrance.

LOCATION: Saguaro National Park East

LENGTH: 8 miles.

RATING: Moderate

CONTACT AGENCY: Saguaro National Park East (520) 733-5153

GETTING THERE: Passenger car. Travel north from KCSP for 9 miles to Interstate 10. Travel west toward Tucson on I-10 for 23 miles to the exit for Vail Road. Stay on this road, which is also signed as Colossal Cave Road, for 3 miles to Camino Loma Alta. Turn left onto Loma Alta and drive north to Old Spanish Trail. Turn left and follow Old Spanish Trail 7.3 miles to Saguaro National Park East. Turn right into the park. From the visitor center, bicycle north on the Cactus Forest Loop Drive.

Saguaro National Park is popular with bikers and hikers

LOOP DRIVE DESCRIPTION:

After passing through the entrance gate, follow the one-way loop drive to the left (north). There are some tight curves and a steep downhill section of road within the first mile. Use caution on the first big hill, which is also narrow and steep and has been the scene of bicycle accidents. This section affords far-reaching scenic vistas of the cactus forest, and beyond, the jagged peaks of the Santa Catalina Mountains. The road winds through a Sonoran Desert landscape of ocotillo, chain-fruit and teddy bear chollas, lacy paloverde trees, and giant saguaros.

2.8 miles from the beginning of the loop drive is the pullout on the right for the Cactus Forest Trail segment that is open to bicycles. This segment bisects the loop drive, returning to the paved road, one-mile southeast of the visitor center.

Continuing on the loop drive, it is another half-mile to the Loma Verde Trailhead on the left. From here the road ascends a high ridgeline, with great views of the saguaro-covered bajadas, or ridges, dropping down from the Rincon Mountains. Along some sections, the road is rimmed with low stone walls, desert plants and wild flowers. Pull off into the Rincon Mountains Overlook to enjoy the view.

At 6 miles is the parking area for Javelina Rocks, an interesting jumble of gigantic boulders. This is a fun place to climb about on the rocks and explore, but be on the alert for rattlesnakes.

A half-mile farther is an intersection. To the left is the Javelina picnic area and the visitor center is to the right. From this junction back to the visitor center, the traffic is two-way. Turning right, it is 0.3 miles to the southern terminus of the bicycle segment of the Cactus Forest Trail, which is signed and has a small parking area. Continuing north, it is one more mile to the visitor center.

TRIP 26

CACTUS FOREST TRAIL

Bicycles are allowed on this 2.5-mile section of the Cactus Forest Trail that is located within the Cactus Forest Loop Drive. You must follow the loop drive to access this trail (See Trip 25). **This is the only trail within the park that is open to bicycles.** *The route passes the remains of an historic lime kiln and has an optional side trip (no bikes) to Lime Falls, a waterfall that flows during rainy periods. The trail may be ridden in either direction, but you may not ride against traffic on the one-way section of the loop drive. Bicyclists are required to yield to all other trail users. Please stop your bicycle and move off the trail if you encounter horses.* **Pets** *are not allowed on any trails within the park.*

DRIVING DISTANCE FROM KCSP: 45 miles to the park entrance.

LOCATION: Saguaro National Park East

LENGTH: 2.8 miles from the visitor center on the paved Cactus Forest Loop Drive, to the Cactus Forest Trail Trailhead. The section of Cactus Forest Trail open to bicycles is 2.5 miles, one way. From the south end of the trail back to the visitor center on the paved loop drive is 1 mile. Total roundtrip distance is 6.3 miles.

RATING: Moderate

CONTACT AGENCY: Saguaro National Park East
(520) 733-5153

GETTING THERE: See Trip 25. Turn right into the park. From the visitor center bicycle north on the Cactus Forest Loop Drive. It is 2.8 miles to the parking area for the Cactus Forest Trail, on the right side of the road.

TRAIL DESCRIPTION:
    2.8 miles from the beginning of the loop drive, the pullout is on the right for the Cactus Forest Trail segment that is open to bicycles. This segment bisects the loop drive,

returning to the paved road, one mile southeast of the visitor center.

The sandy path leading south is almost level as it winds through a Sonoran Desert garden of mesquite trees, prickly pears, chain fruit chollas, and giant saguaros. Looking back and to the east, there are nice views of both the Santa Catalina Mountains and the Rincon Mountains.

One mile from the trailhead is the site of a limestone kiln, constructed around 1880. An interpretive sign tells the story. A short distance farther is the turnoff for Lime Falls. It is 0.4 miles to the falls, which only flow during rainy periods. Bicycles are not allowed on this trail.

Continuing south on the Cactus Forest Trail, the path winds in and out of washes and low hills, with a 100-foot ascent in the last mile. Turn right on the paved road, which has two-way traffic at this point, and it is one mile to the visitors center.

TRIP 27

DESERT ECOLOGY TRAIL

The Desert Ecology Trail is a paved, quarter-mile, barrier-free loop, with occasional resting benches along the route. The trail has interpretive signs explaining plant and animal adaptations in a desert environment. Mid-afternoon temperatures soar above 100 degrees Fahrenheit in the summer months. Wear a hat, use sunscreen and carry water or a cool drink. **Bicycles, horses** *and* **pets** *are not allowed on this trail.*

DRIVING DISTANCE FROM KCSP: 45 miles to the park entrance.

LOCATION: Saguaro National Park East

LENGTH: Quarter-mile loop

RATING: Easy

CONTACT AGENCY: Saguaro National Park East
(520) 733-5153

The paved Ecology Trail has conveniently-placed benches

GETTING THERE: Passenger car. Travel north from KCSP for 9 miles to Interstate 10. Travel west toward Tucson on I-10 for 23 miles to the exit for Vail Road. Stay on this road, which is also signed as Colossal Cave Road, for 3 miles to Camino Loma Alta. Turn left onto Loma Alta and drive north to Old Spanish Trail. Turn left and follow Old Spanish Trail 7.3 miles to Saguaro National Park East. Turn right into the park. From the visitor center drive north on the Cactus Forest Loop Drive for 2.4 miles to the Desert Ecology Trail parking area on the left.

DESCRIPTION:

This pretty, almost-level trail winds through a Sonoran Desert garden of interesting plants and wildlife. Plants such as the graceful paloverde tree, hedgehog and prickly pear cactus and saguaros line the trail. Notice how the large barrel cactus almost always lean to the south – pointing the way to Mexico. Watch for cardinals, and tiny cactus wrens. Gilded flickers and Gila woodpeckers nest in holes in the sides of saguaros. Interpretive signs explain that while most animals are not about during the heat of the day, if you linger in the twilight or return at dawn, you will find the same scene teeming with life.

(TRIP 28)

MICA VIEW LOOP

The Mica View picnic area has picnic tables and grills, a rest room, and a hitching post for horses. The loop trail winds through a forest of older saguaros interspersed with younger cacti that thrive under "nurse trees", such as the green-skinned paloverde. Watch and listen for the abundant bird life in this classic Sonoran Desert environment.

Horses *are allowed on the trail but must access it from a different trailhead. (See GETTING THERE – EQUESTRIANS.)* ***Bicycles*** *are not allowed on this trail. (See the Cactus Forest Loop Drive and Cactus Forest Trail.)* ***Pets*** *are not allowed on any trails within the park.*

DRIVING DISTANCE FROM KCSP: 45 miles to the park entrance.

LOCATION: Saguaro National Park East

LENGTH: 2 miles

RATING: Easy

CONTACT AGENCY: Saguaro National Park East (520) 733-5153

GETTING THERE: Passenger car. Travel north from KCSP for 9 miles to Interstate 10. Travel west toward Tucson on I-10 for 23 miles to the exit for Vail Road. Stay on this road, which is also signed as Colossal Cave Road, for 3 miles to Camino Loma Alta. Turn left onto Loma Alta and drive north to Old Spanish Trail. Turn left and follow Old Spanish Trail 7.3 miles to Saguaro National Park East. Turn right into the park. From the visitor center drive north on Cactus Forest Drive for 2 miles to Mica View Road on the left. Take Mica View Road north a half-mile to the picnic area.

MAP 14
SAGUARO NATIONAL PARK - EAST
28 - Mica View Loop
29 - Loma Verde/Pink Hill/Squeeze Pen Loop

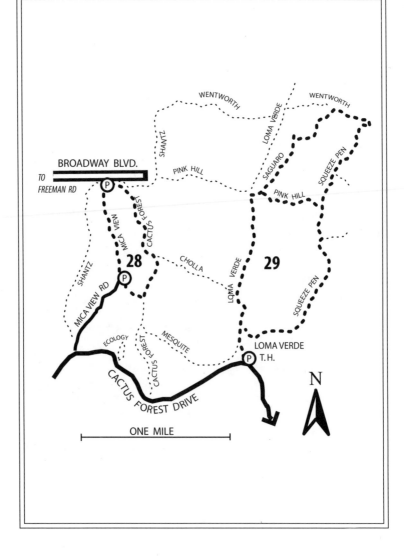

EQUESTRIANS: Instead of turning into the park from Old Spanish Trail, continue for 0.1 miles to a junction with Freeman Road. As Old Spanish Trail curves to the left, take the Freeman Road fork to the right and drive for 2.8 miles to Broadway. Turn right on Broadway and drive 0.6 miles to the Broadway Trailhead on the right. There is a loop at the end of the road to turn horse trailers.

DESCRIPTION:

The Mica View Trail leaves from the north end of the Mica View picnic area. The path is wide, level, sandy, and lined with an array of Sonoran Desert plants: big teddy bear chollas, barrel cactus, graceful paloverde trees, mesquite trees, prickly pear and saguaros.

As you approach Broadway Boulevard, 0.7 miles from the picnic area, turn right onto the Shantz Trail, then right again onto Cactus Forest Trail. (Equestrians begin the loop here, from Broadway.) The route affords far-reaching views of oak-covered Tanque Verde Peak, and beyond, the higher profile of Mica Mountain. Mica Mountain is named for the shiny mineral deposits found there, sometimes called "fools gold".

The trail passes through a cactus garden of prickly pear

Prickly pear fruit is a food source for birds and rodents

and cholla. Watch for two huge barrel cactus that are leaning into the trail. While most barrel cactus lean south or southeast, these two are leaning to the southwest. After crossing Javelina Wash, watch for Arizona's state tree, a blue paloverde.

Stay on Cactus Forest Trail until it intercepts Mica View Trail, southeast of the picnic area. Turn right onto Mica View Trail and re-cross Javelina Wash, under a canopy of mesquite trees, to return to the Mica View Picnic Area. Equestrians, as you enter the area, a sign directs horses to a trail that circles around the perimeter of the picnic area, to a hitching post on the north side.

TRIP 29

LOMA VERDE / PINK HILL / SQUEEZE PEN LOOP or LOMA VERDE / SAGUARO / SQUEEZE PEN LOOP

This trip offers the choice of a 3.3-mile loop or a 5.1-mile loop. The route passes by the site of an old copper mine, makes an easy climb up Pink Hill for a panoramic view of the cactus forest, and passes by some magnificent saguaros.

__Horses__ are allowed on the trail but must access it from the Broadway Trailhead. See GETTING THERE – EQUESTRIANS. __Bicycles__ are not allowed on this trail. (See the Cactus Forest Loop Drive and Cactus Forest Trail.) __Pets__ are not allowed on any trails within the park.

DRIVING DISTANCE FROM KCSP: 45 miles to the park entrance.

LOCATION: Saguaro National Park East

LENGTH: 3.3 mile or 5.1 mile loop

RATING: Moderate

CONTACT AGENCY: Saguaro National Park East
(520) 733-5153

GETTING THERE: Passenger car. Travel north from KCSP for 9 miles to Interstate 10. Travel west toward Tucson on I-10 for 23 miles to the exit for Vail Road. Stay on this road, which is also signed as Colossal Cave Road, for 3 miles to Camino Loma Alta. Turn left onto Loma Alta and drive north to Old Spanish Trail. Turn left and follow Old Spanish Trail 7.3 miles to Saguaro National Park East. Turn right into the park. From the visitor center drive north on Cactus Forest Drive for 3.5 miles to the Loma Verde Trailhead.

EQUESTRIANS: Instead of turning into the park from Old Spanish Trail, continue for 0.1 miles to a junction with Freeman Road. As Old Spanish Trail curves to the left, take the Freeman Road fork to the right and drive for 2.8 miles to Broadway. Turn right on Broadway and drive 0.6 miles to the Broadway Trailhead on the right. There is a loop at the end of the road to turn horse trailers. Follow the Shantz Trail left (east) for 0.3 miles to connect to the Pink Hill Trail. Continue east on Pink Hill Trail for 0.8 miles to the Loma Verde Trail.

DESCRIPTION:

From the trailhead on Cactus Forest Drive, the Loma Verde Trail heads north through a mesquite woodland scattered with saguaros and barrel cactus. In early spring watch for the magenta blooms of the hedgehog cactus. Passing a turnoff for the Mesquite Trail on the left, follow the Loma Verde Trail as it drops down into Monument Wash.

Just after crossing the wash is a junction with the Squeeze Pen Trail, our return route. Stay left, continuing north on the Loma Verde Trail. This is a pleasant, level, sandy trail.

The trail crosses the wash again, then follows along the right bank to a junction with Cholla Trail. Continue north on the Loma Verde Trail to the site of the old mine. Here an interpretive sign tells the history of the Loma Verde Mine, which began operation in 1901.

1.2 miles from the trailhead is the junction with the Pink Hill Trail. This is where equestrians join the loop, coming in from the Broadway Trailhead. Leaving the Loma Verde Trail, follow the Pink Hill Trail east, as it climbs a reddish-colored

Equestrians are permitted on many trails in Saguaro National Park

slope. The hill affords magnificent views of the cactus forest and the Santa Catalina Mountains.

For the shorter 3.3-mile loop, continue on the Pink Hill Trail east for 0.7 miles to the Squeeze Pen Trail junction and turn right (south). The name of this trail comes from ranching days. Squeeze pens are structures that are designed to hold cattle that need to be branded or given medical attention.

Following the Squeeze Pen Trail, there are nice views of the sloping saguaro-covered bajadas, or ridgelines dropping down from the Rincon Mountains on the east. As you follow the trail, note the variety of plant life: palo verdes, ocotillo, teddy bear cholla, and the park's namesake, giant saguaros, line the trail.

One mile from the Pink Hill junction, the trail crosses a large wash. 0.3 miles farther it crosses again. Look to the right for an ancient, massive saguaro cactus. The trail swings west and re-enters a mesquite bosque. Turn left onto the Loma Verde Trail to return to the trailhead. (Equestrians turn right onto the Loma Verde Trail to complete the loop back to the Pink Hill Trail junction. Return to the Broadway Trailhead.)

For a longer scenic loop (5.1 total miles): Instead of following the Pink Hill Trail east to the Squeeze Pen Trail, turn left (north) onto the Saguaro Trail, at the top of Pink Hill. The trail winds and rolls over and around low hills in an easy, mostly down-hill grade.

The trail crosses a wash, which it then follows for 0.2 miles. Watch closely for the place where the trail leaves the wash on the right (east) bank. Shortly after leaving the wash the trail comes to an unsigned junction with another well-used wash route. Continue northeast across the junction, climbing uphill. Stones have been placed to form low, wide steps that do not pose a problem for horses.

Continue on the Saguaro Trail to the junction with the Wentworth Trail. Follow the Wentworth Trail for 0.3 miles to the Kennedy Trail. Turn right (south) onto the Kennedy trail, and in 60 feet, turn right again onto the Squeeze Pen Trail. Heading sothwest the trail winds up and down through several small arroyos. It is 0.9 miles to the Pink Hill junction. From the junction, follow the Sqeeze Pen Trail back to Loma Verde Trail. Turn left to the trailhead parking area. (Equestrians turn right onto the Loma Verde Trail to return to the Broadway Trailhead.)

Rider and pack mule head for the high country

SAGUARO / RINCON MOUNTAIN WILDERNESS

The wilderness of Saguaro National Park is bordered on the north, south and east by the Rincon Mountain Wilderness and Coronado National Forest. While access to Saguaro National Park East's visitor center is on the west, or Tucson side of the Rincons, the Turkey Creek Trailhead leads into the Rincons from an area on the east side of the Rincons, known as Happy Valley.

The Saguaro Wilderness is extremely rugged with deep canyons and high rocky ridges. The remoteness of the area and the steep trails make for a strenuous and challenging adventure, far from the more frequently used trails on the east side of the range.

The mixed conifer-topped summit of the Rincons offers a delightful contrast to other Arizona Sky islands. While most ranges are crowned with high, jagged peaks and narrow wind-swept ridgelines, the crest of the Rincons has a lush, park-like atmosphere.

Manning Camp, a historic log cabin dating back to 1905, sits atop the mountain at 8,000 feet. The cabin, which is still in use, now serves as headquarters for a backcountry campground and fire crew station. From Manning Camp, an extensive trail system offers a variety of treks through cool woodlands and flower-dotted meadows, and great bird watching opportunities for higher-elevation species. There are streams, pools, and scenic overlooks with far-reaching views in all directions.

With advance arrangements for transportation, hikers can travel up from the east side of the range and make their descent down the west side, to the park's visitor center. A trans-mountain hike would require a minimum of two days.

MAP 15
SAGUARO / RINCON
MOUNTAIN WILDERNESS
30 - Turkey Creek to Manning Camp (Arizona Trail)

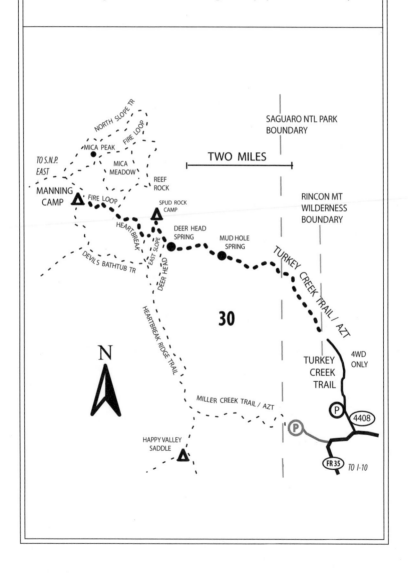

NORTH SLOPE TR

FIRE LOOP

MICA PEAK

MICA MEADOW

TO S.N.P. EAST

REEF ROCK

MANNING CAMP

FIRE LOOP

SPUD ROCK CAMP

HEARTBREAK

DEER HEAD SPRING

MUD HOLE SPRING

EAST SLOPE

DEVILS BATHTUB TR

DEER HEAD

HEARTBREAK RIDGE TRAIL

30

SAGUARO NTL PARK BOUNDARY

TWO MILES

RINCON MT WILDERNESS BOUNDARY

TURKEY CREEK TRAIL / AZT

N

MILLER CREEK TRAIL / AZT

TURKEY CREEK TRAIL

4WD ONLY

P

4408

HAPPY VALLEY SADDLE

P

FR 35   *TO I-10*

(TRIP 30)

TURKEY CREEK TO MANNING CAMP

Trip 30 is the most difficult hike described in this guide and requires a minimum of two days to complete. 3 or 4 days is preferable, to enjoy and explore the high-mountain forests, meadows and scenic vistas of the Rincon Mountains. Manning Camp is a remote area, not accessible by road. Permits (free) are required in advance. It may be a sweltering 100 degrees at the beginning of the hike, and a frigid 50 degrees or less on top of the mountain, so be prepared. The Rincons may be snowed in, in the winter months. For information on trails, water availability, camping, regulations and permits, contact Saguaro National Park.

Horses *are allowed on this trail and in campgrounds, but MUST have a permit in advance. The trail may pose problems for all but the most experienced and fit trail animals. Some sections of trail are very steep while other sections are deeply worn and narrow, posing a danger to horse's legs. Heat exhaustion can kill livestock. Allow animals frequent rest stops.*

Bicycles *may travel for one and a half miles up the old road but are NOT allowed beyond the first gate which is the Rincon Mountain Wilderness boundary.* ***Pets*** *are not allowed on trails within the National Park.*

At time of printing this trip is still considered to be a part of the state-wide Arizona Trail. At some time in the future, the route of the AZT may be changed from an eastern to a southern approach.

DRIVING DISTANCE FROM KCSP: 31 miles

LOCATION: Happy Valley, within Coronado National Forest, to Manning Camp, located in Saguaro National Park

LENGTH: 17.5 miles round trip. (14.5 miles if you 4WD to the end of the road.)

RATING: Most difficult with an elevation gain of almost 4,000 feet.

CONTACT AGENCY: Saguaro National Park East (520) 733-5153. Coronado National Forest, Santa Catalina Ranger district (520) 749-8700

GETTING THERE: Passenger car, although the road may be washboarded and crosses drainages that could be a problem in wet weather. Travel north from KCSP for 9 miles to Interstate 10. Travel west toward Tucson on I-10 for 5 miles to the exit (297) for Mescal and J-Six Ranch Road. Turn right and travel north on Mescal Road.

After two and a half miles the pavement ends and the road becomes FR 35. Look to the left for a glimpse of a Western movie set that is owned by Old Tucson Studios. Many films including *The Quick and The Dead, Tombstone,* and the TV series *Legends* have been filmed here. The movie set is on private property and is not open to the public.

From I-10 it is 15.8 miles to a signed turnoff for the Miller Creek Trailhead. Miller Creek is a very steep but scenic hiking route (no horses) that affords access to 8,482-foot Rincon Peak and can also be used to reach Manning Camp.

Continue past the Miller Creek turnoff for another 0.4 miles, watching for FR 4408 on the left. Turn left on FR 4408 and drive 0.3 miles to a gate. From the gate it is 0.2 miles to the Turkey Creek trailhead. Just beyond the gate there are shady level areas under huge sycamore trees, a seasonal creek, and room for parking horse trailers.

DESCRIPTION:

The Turkey Creek Trail climbs north on a steep 4WD road, as it ascends a long, open ridge with views of the massive Rincons looming to the west. Hikers who wish to drive the one and a half miles to the end of the road may do so with 4WD only and bicycles are also permitted. This section of road is NOT open to horse trailers. The distinctive cliff face known as Reef Rock is visible, and just below, the bright green of aspen trees marks Spud Rock Spring. To the left is the long line of Heartbreak Ridge and 8,482-foot Rincon Peak.

One and a half miles from the trailhead the road ends and a trail begins in a rocky area, continuing along a ridge. The first gate marks the wilderness boundary. The trail winds over and around cactus and manzanita-covered foothills for another 0.7 miles before dipping down to the gate which

Tall pines and cool shade await the Manning Camp visitor

marks the boundary between Coronado National Forest and Saguaro National Park. Along this stretch, charred tree stumps remain from the fire that swept through the area in July of 1994.

In a grassy saddle, three and a half miles from the trailhead, a sign-in box reminds trail users that permits are required for overnight stays. From the saddle, a series of rock steps lead travelers on a long, steep switchbacking ascent up the mountain. Equestrians may want to lead their animals through some of the narrow, deeply worn sections of trail.

6 miles from the trailhead the route passes by a spring, shaded by large oaks and ponderosa pine trees. At just over 7,000 feet, Deer Head Spring is an inviting place to take a break. Above Deer Head Spring is a junction of trails. Travel north (right) on Deer Head Spring Trail toward the Spud Rock Campground. Entering a grove of aspen trees, the trail arrives at a junction.

Take the East Slope Trail left, a very short distance to Switchback Trail. Turn right and follow Switchback Trail, watching for the occasional views of the San Pedro River Valley and the Galiuro Mountains to the east.

At 0.3 miles is another junction. Veer right for 0.7 miles on Heartbreak Ridge Trail to the Fireloop Trail. Continue west (left) on Fireloop Trail to Manning Camp. A short distance from camp, the route joins the Mica Mountain Trail.

Manning Camp makes a great base camp for day hikes to Mica Mountain, the Devil's Bathtub, loop trips and scenic overlooks. At 8,000 feet, you are on top of the world. The little waterfall behind the cabin is a good place to listen for the flute-like song of the Hermit Thrush.

Southeast Arizona's "sky islands" are typically populated with pondrosa pine and Douglas fir

GPS COORDINATES

All of the trails described in this book were either hiked or ridden by the author. A global positioning system (GPS) was used to calculate the mileage and to create the maps for many of the trails. In a few cases, the mileage for some of the older, established trails was taken from information provided by the managing agencies.

The following GPS coordinates are provided for the reader's convenience. Units are degrees, minutes, and hundredths of minutes.

Hike	Waypoint Description	Latitude	Longitude
1	**Foothills Loop Trail**		
	Trailhead	N31° 50.16'	W110° 21.01'
	Viewpoint	N31° 50.66'	W110° 21.13'
2	**Guindani Trail**		
	Trailhead	N31° 50.13'	W110° 21.39'
	Cottonwood Saddle Junction	N31° 50.48'	W110° 22.74'
	Gate	N31° 50.08'	W110° 22.62'
3	**Presidio Santa Cruz de Terrenate**		
	Trailhead	N31° 44.81'	W110° 13.06'
	Presidio	N31° 44.98'	W110° 12.18'
4	**Fairbank River Loop Trail**		
	Fairbank	N31° 43.50'	W110° 11.32'
	Millsite	N31° 44.41'	W110° 11.47'
	Junction	N31° 44.78'	W110° 11.61'
5	**Murray Springs Clovis Site**		
	Trailhead	N31° 34.26'	W110° 10.91'
6	**San Pedro House - Kingfisher Pond Loop**		
	SP House	N31° 32.89'	W110° 08.49'
	Green King Fisher Pond	N31° 32.62'	W110° 08.05'
7	**Slavin Gulch**		
	Trailhead	N31° 52.72'	W110° 01.58'
	Gulch entrance	N31° 53.28'	W110° 00.82'
	Mine	N31° 54.49'	W109° 59.64'
8	**Council Rocks**		
	Trailhead	N31° 54.65'	W110° 02.36'
	Pictographs	N31° 54.48'	W110° 02.34'

Hike	Waypoint Description	Latitude	Longitude
9	**Cochise Trail #279 - West Stronghold**		
	Trailhead, West Stronghold	N31° 55.77'	W109° 59.81'
	Saddle	N31° 55.27'	W109° 59.06'
	Half Moon Tank	N31° 54.74'	W109° 58.69'
	Trailhead, East Stronghold	N31° 55.51'	W109° 58.04'
10	**Brown Canyon Trail**		
	Trailhead	N31° 27.83'	W110° 17.49'
	Spring	N31° 27.48'	W110° 19.24'
11	**Ramsey Canyon Preserve - Hamburg Trail**		
	Trailhead	N31° 26.80'	W110° 18.50'
	Overlook	N31° 26.43'	W110° 18.93'
12	**Perimeter Trail**		
	Trailhead, Carr Canyon Rd	N31° 26.95'	W110° 17.05'
	Trailhead, Miller Rd	N31° 25.58'	W110° 15.44'
13	**Clark Spring / John Cooper Trails**		
	Trailhead, Miller Rd	N31° 25.00'	W110° 16.54'
	Trailhead, Carr Canyon Rd	N31° 26.16'	W110° 16.47'
14	**Carr Peak Trail**		
	Trailhead	N31° 25.67'	W110° 17.45'
	Carr Peak	N31° 24.78'	W110° 18.27'
15	**Miller Canyon Trail to Miller Peak**		
	Trailhead	N31° 25.00'	W110° 16.54'
	Bathtub Spring	N31° 24.34'	W110° 18.80'
	Miller Peak	N31° 23.56'	W110° 17.59'
16	**Coronado Cave Trail**		
	Trailhead	N31° 20.76'	W110° 15.23'
	Cave	N31° 21.06'	W110° 15.64'
17	**Joe's Canyon Trail**		
	Trailhead	N31° 20.72'	W110° 15.27'
	Yaqui Ridge Junction	N31° 20.58'	W110° 16.67'
	Montezuma Pass	N31° 21.02'	W110° 17.11'
18	**Yaqui Ridge (AZT)**		
	Trailhead Montezuma Pass	N31° 21.02'	W110° 17.11'
	Junction	N31° 20.58'	W110° 16.67'
	US/Mexico Boundary	N31° 20.00'	W110° 16.93'
19	**Coronado Peak Trail**		
	Trailhead, Montezuma Pass	N31° 21.02'	W110° 17.11'
	Coronado Peak	N31° 20.75'	W110° 17.08'

Hike	Waypoint Description	Latitude	Longitude
20	**South Road to the Empire Ranch**		
	South Road	N31° 42.09'	W110° 35.45'
	Empire Ranch	N31° 47.12'	W110° 38.54'
21	**Oak Tree Canyon to Empire Ranch (AZT)**		
	Trailhead, Oak Tree Canyon	N31° 48.65'	W110° 42.69'
	Empire Ranch	N31° 47.12'	W110° 38.54'
22	**The Ditch (AZT)**		
	Trailhead, Gardner Canyon Rd	N31° 43.19'	W110° 45.21'
	FR 785	N31° 42.41'	W110° 46.50'
23	**Gardner Canyon to Kentucky Camp (AZT)**		
	Trailhead, Gardner Canyon Rd	N31° 43.19'	W110° 45.21'
	Leaves ridgeline	N31° 43.90'	W110° 43.96'
	Kentucky Camp	N31° 44.66'	W110° 44.49'
24	**Kentucky Camp to Oak Tree Canyon (AZT)**		
	Kentucky Camp	N31° 44.66'	W110° 44.49'
	Crossing, Box Canyon Rd	N31° 47.56'	W110° 44.83'
	Oak Tree Canyon	N31° 48.54'	W110° 42.66'
25	**Cactus Forest Loop Drive**		
	Start/End	N32° 10.80'	W110° 44.13'
	Mica Road Junction	N32° 12.21'	W110° 43.80'
26	**Cactus Forest Trail**		
	Trailhead, North End	N32° 11.97'	W110° 43.32'
	Trailhead, South End	N32° 10.27'	W110° 43.76'
27	**Desert Ecology Trail**		
	Trailhead	N32° 12.19'	W110° 43.50'
28	**Mica View Loop**		
	Trailhead	N32° 12.71'	W110° 43.47'
	Broadway	N32° 13.23'	W110° 43.57'
29	**Loma Verde / Pink Hill / Squeeze Pen Loop**		
	Trailhead	N32° 12.19'	W110° 42.58'
	Pink Hill Junction	N32° 13.17'	W110° 42.55'
	Wentworth Trail	N32° 13.67'	W110° 41.97'
30	**Turkey Creek to Manning Camp (AZT)**		
	Trailhead	N32° 09.48'	W110° 28.54'
	Gate	N32° 11.49'	W110° 29.69'
	Manning Camp	N32° 12.57'	W110° 33.24'